Call to Faith

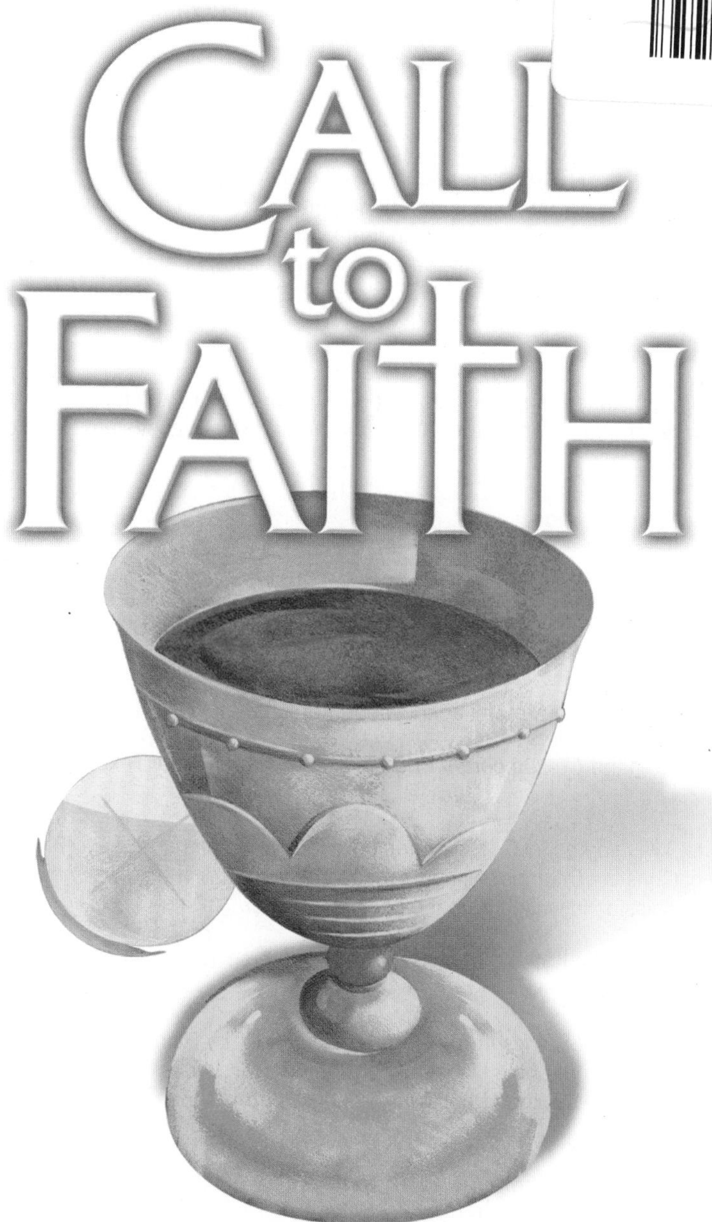

GRADE 2

School

Our Sunday Visitor

Curriculum Division

www.osvcurriculum.com

The Subcommittee on the Catechism, United States Conference of Catholic Bishops, has found this catechetical series, © 2009 Edition, to be in conformity with the *Catechism of the Catholic Church.*

Nihil Obstat
Rev. Richard L. Schaefer

Imprimatur
✠ Most Rev. Thomas Wenski
Bishop of Orlando
December 14, 2007

The Imprimatur is an official declaration that a book or pamphlet is free of doctrinal or moral error. No implication is contained therein that anyone who granted the Imprimatur agrees with the contents, opinions, or statements expressed.

Write:
Our Sunday Visitor Curriculum Division
Our Sunday Visitor, Inc.
200 Noll Plaza, Huntington, Indiana 46750

For permission to reprint copyrighted material, grateful acknowledgment is made to the following sources:

American Bible Society: Scriptures from the *Contemporary English Version of the Bible*. Text copyright © 1999 by American Bible Society.

Confraternity of Christian Doctrine, Washington, D.C.: Scriptures from the *New American Bible*. Text copyright © 1991, 1986, 1970 by the Confraternity of Christian Doctrine. All rights reserved. No part of the *New American Bible* may be used or reproduced in any form, without permission in writing from the copyright owner.

CRC Publications: Lyrics from "For Health and Strength" by Bert Polman. (verse 1, traditional). Lyrics © 1994 by CRC Publications.

Hope Publishing Co., Carol Stream, IL 60188: Lyrics from "We Are the Church" by Richard Avery and Donald Marsh. Lyrics © 1972 by Hope Publishing Co. Lyrics from "Lord of the Dance" by Sydney Carter. Lyrics © 1963 by Stainer & Bell Ltd. Lyrics from "Spirit-Friend" by Tom Colvin. Lyrics © 1969 by Hope Publishing Co. Lyrics from "Jesus' Hands Were Kind Hands" by Margaret Cropper. Lyrics © 1979 by Stainer & Bell Ltd.

The English translation of the Psalm Responses from *Lectionary for Mass* © 1969, 1981, 1997, International Commission on English in the Liturgy Corporation (ICEL); the English translation of the Act of Contrition from *Rite of Penance* © 1974, ICEL; excerpts from the English translation of *Eucharistic Prayers for Masses with Children* © 1975, ICEL; the English translation of the Prayer to the Guardian Angel from *A Book of Prayers* © 1982, ICEL; excerpts from the English translation of *The Roman Missal* © 2010, ICEL. All rights reserved.

Additional acknowledgments appear on page 326.

Call to Faith School Grade 2 Student Edition
ISBN: 978-0-15-902283-2
Item Number: CU1379

6 7 8 9 10 11 12 13 015016 18 17 16 15 14
Webcrafters, Inc., Madison, WI, USA; October 2014; Job # 119255

Grade 2 Contents

Catholic Source Book

About Your Book

Your book has many things in it. It can help you learn more about your faith and people who live their faith. It will also show you different ways to celebrate your faith.

Activity Connect Your Faith

Seek and Find To get to know your book, look for the pictures in the signs below. Write down where you find each of them.

Page ____________

Page ____________

Page ____________

Page ____________

Page ____________

Page ____________

A Call to Faith

Gather

Pray the Sign of the Cross together.

Leader: The Lord be with you.

All: And with your spirit.

Leader: Let us pray.

Bow your heads as the leader prays.

All: Amen.

Listen to God's Word

Reader: A reading from the holy Gospel according to Matthew.

Read Mathew 4:18–22.

The Gospel of the Lord.

All: Praise to you, Lord Jesus Christ.

Reflect

How did the fishermen change that day? How does Jesus call you today?

Prayer of the Faithful

Leader: Lord, you called Simon and Andrew, and they followed you. They had faith in you and your works. With that same faith, we offer you our prayers.

Respond to each prayer with these words.

All: Lord, hear our prayer.

Signing of Foreheads

Silently pray to the Holy Spirit asking for strength to share God's word with all you meet.

Then come forward as your name is called. The leader will mark your forehead with the Sign of the Cross.

Leader: (Name), may your actions show that you have answered Jesus' call to follow him.

All: Amen.

Go Forth!

Leader: Let us begin this new year with all the joy and love that comes from Christ.

All: Thanks be to God.

Sing together.

We are called to act with justice,
we are called to love tenderly,
we are called to serve one another;
to walk humbly with God!

Special Days

Your family shares special days together. You may have big celebrations that include lots of people. You may celebrate birthdays and holidays with friends and people you love.

The Church shares special times together, too. These special times are called seasons. The Church's seasons celebrate events in the lives of Jesus, Mary, and saints.

Words and Actions
Hands are raised in prayer.
Heads are bowed in silence.
The Cross is honored by kneeling in front of it or kissing it.
The sign of Christ's peace is offered with a handshake.
The Sign of the Cross is marked on foreheads, hearts, and lips.

During the year, your class will use these words and actions to celebrate the different seasons.

The Church Year

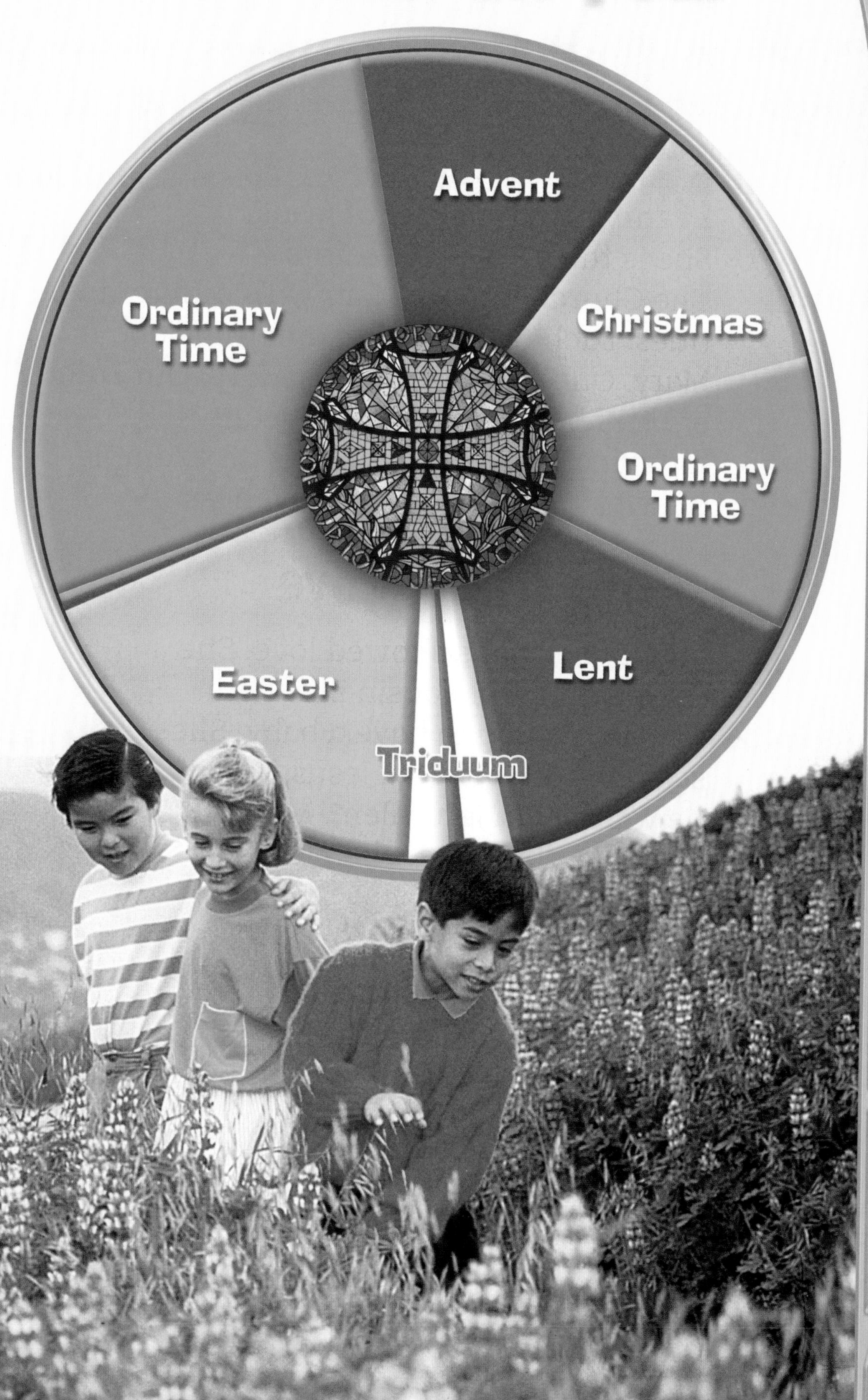

Mother of Mercy

Mary is the mother of Jesus. She is the greatest of saints. The Church honors Mary with different titles. Each title tells us something about Mary. One of these titles is Mary, Our Lady of Mercy. To show mercy means to be forgiving and loving. Mary is an example of love, kindness, and forgiveness.

Acting Out of Love

Mary's actions showed love. She stayed with her cousin Elizabeth who was going to have a baby. She searched for her Son, Jesus, when he was lost in Jerusalem. Mary stayed at the cross when Jesus died. She forgave those who hurt him, as Jesus did.

Mary shows us how to love and forgive others even when we think they have made a mistake.

? What is a way that you can show mercy to others?

Celebrate Mary

Gather

Pray the Sign of the Cross together.

Leader: Blessed be God.

All: Blessed be God forever.

Leader: Let us pray.

Bow your heads as the leader prays.

All: Amen.

Listen to God's Word

Leader: A reading from the holy Gospel according to Luke.

Read Luke 1:39–42, 45.

The Gospel of the Lord.

All: Praise to you, Lord Jesus Christ.

Reflect

What does Elizabeth say to Mary?

What is one way Mary showed her love?

Sing together.

For your gracious blessing,
for your wondrous word,
for your loving kindness,
we give thanks, O God.

"For Your Gracious Blessing" Traditional

Heads Bowed in Prayer

Bow your heads and think about Mary's love and kindness. Then pray together.

Leader: Hail Mary, full of grace,
the Lord is with you!
Blessed are you among
women,
and blessed is the fruit of
your womb, Jesus.

All: Holy Mary, Mother of God,
pray for us sinners,
now and at the hour of
our death. Amen.

Go Forth!

Leader: Go forth to love and serve the Lord,
as Mary did throughout her life.

All: Thanks be to God.

Sing together.

For your gracious blessing,
for your wondrous word,
for your loving kindness,
we give thanks, O God.

"For Your Gracious Blessing" Traditional

Showing Mercy

People who show mercy notice what is happening to others. They try to see things from the other person's point of view. Merciful people think of what others need and try to help.

Who do you know who needs something? How can you show mercy?

ACTIVITY

Act Out a Mercy Prayer

Work together with your class. Make gestures to go with this Mercy Prayer. Show what the words mean. Say the mercy prayer every morning.

Jesus, have mercy on me.
Mary, help me show mercy
to others today. Amen.

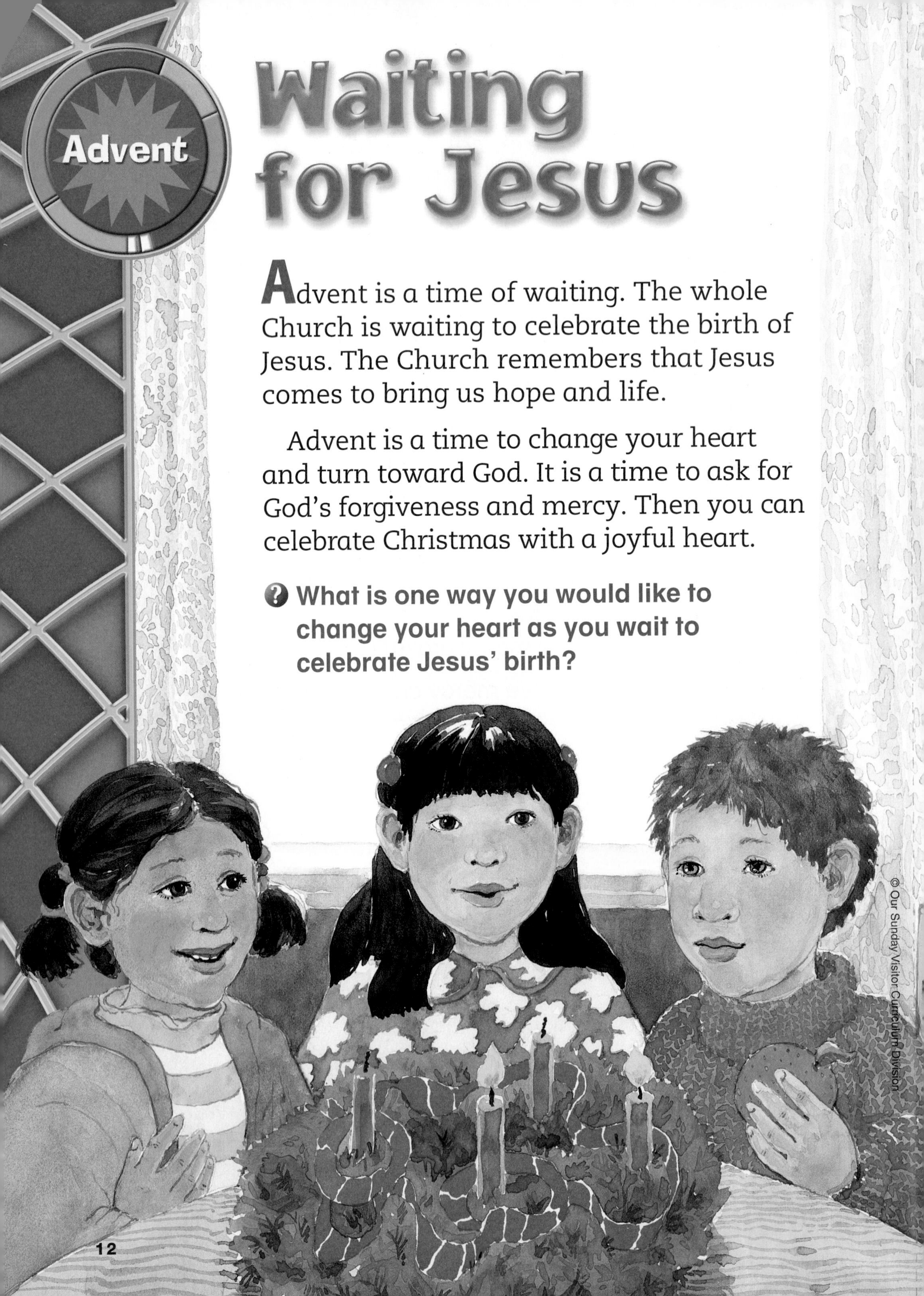

Waiting for Jesus

Advent is a time of waiting. The whole Church is waiting to celebrate the birth of Jesus. The Church remembers that Jesus comes to bring us hope and life.

Advent is a time to change your heart and turn toward God. It is a time to ask for God's forgiveness and mercy. Then you can celebrate Christmas with a joyful heart.

? What is one way you would like to change your heart as you wait to celebrate Jesus' birth?

Celebrate Advent

Gather

Sing together.

Come, O Lord, change our hearts!
Emmanuel, God is with us.

Pray the Sign of the Cross together.

Leader: Our help is in the name of the Lord.

All: Who made heaven and earth.

Leader: Lord, you came to gather all peoples in peace.
Lord, have mercy.

All: Lord, have mercy.

Leader: Lord, you came to show us how to be holy.
Christ, have mercy.

All: Christ, have mercy.

Leader: Lord, you will come again in glory to save your people.
Lord, have mercy.

All: Lord, have mercy.

Leader: May God have mercy on us, forgive us our sins, and bring us to everlasting life.

All: Amen.

Listen to God's Word

Leader: A reading from the holy Gospel according to Mark.

Read Mark 1:14–15.

The Gospel of the Lord.

All: Praise to you, Lord Jesus Christ.

Pray Around the Advent Wreath

Sit in silence before the Advent wreath. Think of a way you will change your heart during Advent.

Leader: Glory to the Father, and to the Son, and to the Holy Spirit:

All: As it was in the beginning, is now, and will be forever. Amen.

Go Forth!

Leader: Let us go forth to love and serve the Lord by showing kindness to one another.

All: Thanks be to God.

Closer to God

Sometimes you may forget that God is near. You may make choices that draw you away from God. Advent is a good time to remember God's love for you. It is a time to draw closer to him.

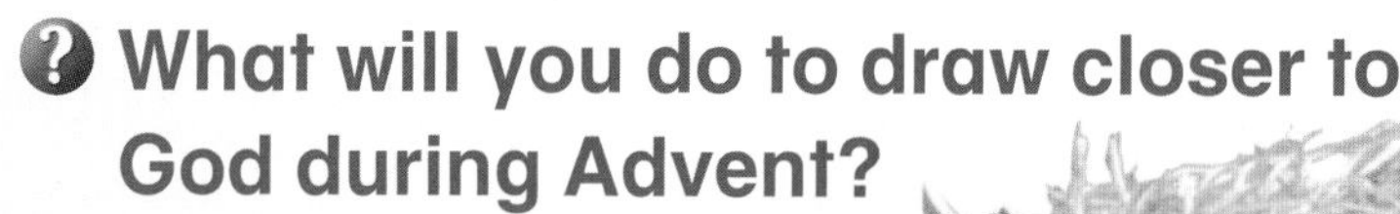

What will you do to draw closer to God during Advent?

ACTIVITY

Fill the Manger

On a separate sheet of paper, draw a manger. Underneath it write what you will do to show your love for others during Advent. Every time you show your love, draw a piece of straw in the manger. By Christmas, you will have a soft bed for the baby Jesus.

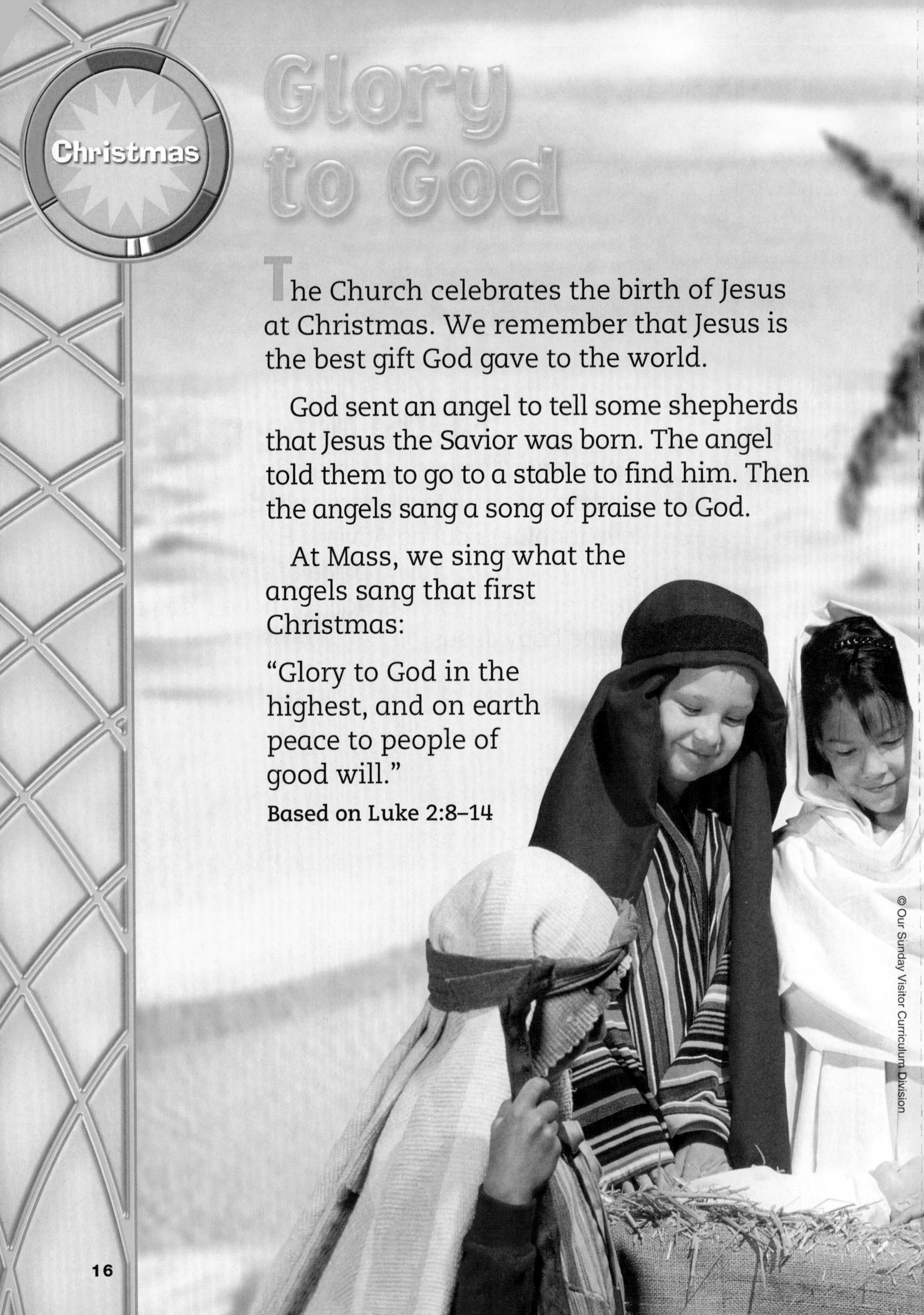

Christmas

Glory to God

The Church celebrates the birth of Jesus at Christmas. We remember that Jesus is the best gift God gave to the world.

God sent an angel to tell some shepherds that Jesus the Savior was born. The angel told them to go to a stable to find him. Then the angels sang a song of praise to God.

At Mass, we sing what the angels sang that first Christmas:

"Glory to God in the highest, and on earth peace to people of good will."

Based on Luke 2:8–14

Celebrate Christmas

Gather

Sing together.

He came down that we may have love;
He came down that we may have love;
He came down that we may have love,
Hallelujah for ever more.

"He Came Down" Cameroon traditional

Pray the Sign of the Cross together.

Leader: Blessed be the name of the Lord.

All: Now and forever.

Leader: Let us pray.

Bow your heads as the leader prays.

All: Amen.

Listen to God's Word

Leader: A reading from the holy Gospel according to Luke.

Read Luke 2:8–14.

The Gospel of the Lord.

All: Praise to you, Lord Jesus Christ.

Pray Before the Crèche

Come forward and kneel before the crèche.

Leader: God, our Father, we thank you for the gift of Jesus, your Son.

All: We praise you, we bless you, we thank you.

Leader: We thank you for all the gifts of creation.

All: We praise you, we bless you, we thank you.

Leader: We ask your blessing on all your people.

All: We praise you, we bless you, we thank you.

Go Forth!

Leader: Go forth to sing of God's glory and to share his peace with others.

All: Thanks be to God.

Share the Good News

The shepherds in the fields were people of faith. They believed the good news the angel told them about Jesus.

After they saw the baby Jesus, they shared the good news with others.

? What other good news about Jesus do you know? Who can you tell?

ACTIVITY

Make a Good News Banner

The things you say and do can help people learn more about Jesus. As his follower, your good actions share the good news of Jesus' love. With a partner make a list of actions that show love. Then write them on a banner. Decorate your banner and hang it in the classroom.

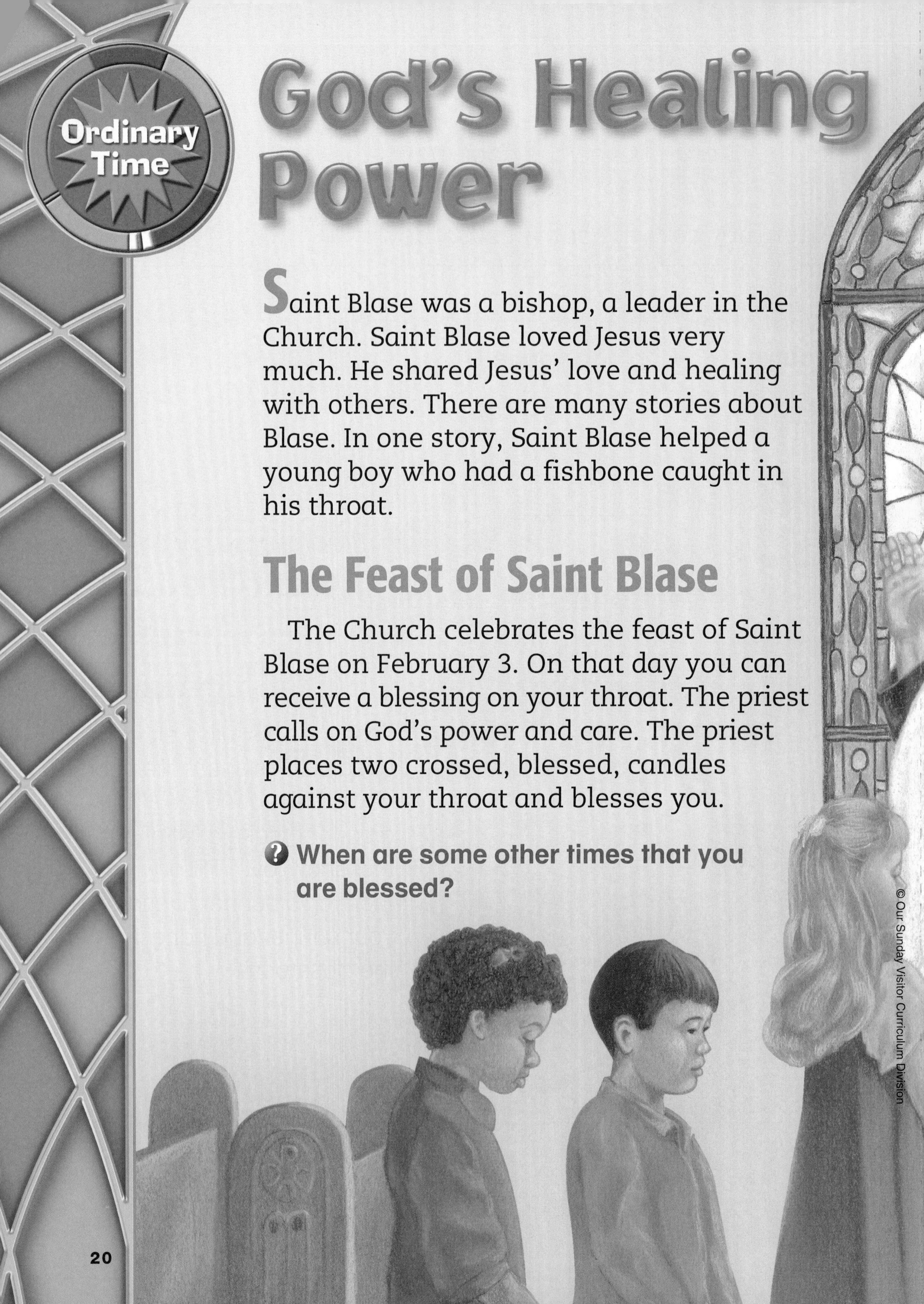

Ordinary Time

God's Healing Power

Saint Blase was a bishop, a leader in the Church. Saint Blase loved Jesus very much. He shared Jesus' love and healing with others. There are many stories about Blase. In one story, Saint Blase helped a young boy who had a fishbone caught in his throat.

The Feast of Saint Blase

The Church celebrates the feast of Saint Blase on February 3. On that day you can receive a blessing on your throat. The priest calls on God's power and care. The priest places two crossed, blessed, candles against your throat and blesses you.

When are some other times that you are blessed?

Celebrate Healing

Gather

Pray the Sign of the Cross together.

Leader: Our help is in the name of the Lord.

All: Who made heaven and earth.

Leader: Let us pray.

Bow your heads as the leader prays.

All: Amen.

Listen to God's Word

Leader: A reading from the holy Gospel according to Matthew.

Read Matthew 8:14–17.

The Gospel of the Lord.

All: Praise to you, Lord Jesus Christ.

Prayer of the Faithful

Leader: Let us pray for all who are sick and suffering, and for all those who care for them.

After each prayer, answer together.

All: Lord, hear our prayer.

Leader: Let us pray in the words that Jesus taught us.

All: Our Father . . .

Blessing of Throats

Sing together.

For health and strength and
  daily food,
For neighbors, friends,
  and family,
We give you thanks, O God.
For faith and hope and
  loving care.

"For Health and Strength" © 1994, CRC Publications

As you sing, walk forward singing to receive a blessing on your throat.

Leader: Through the intercession of Saint Blase, bishop and martyr, may God deliver you from every disease of the throat and from every other illness. In the name of the Father, and of the Son, and of the Holy Spirit.

All: Amen.

Go Forth!

Leader: Let us go forth like Saint Blase, to bring God's healing Spirit to everyone we meet.

All: **Thanks be to God.**

Blessings

A blessing is a reminder that God loves you and that God is near. When you receive a blessing, you can thank God for his goodness to you. When you give a blessing, you remind others of God's love for them.

What are some other times that you have received a blessing?

When do you bless others?

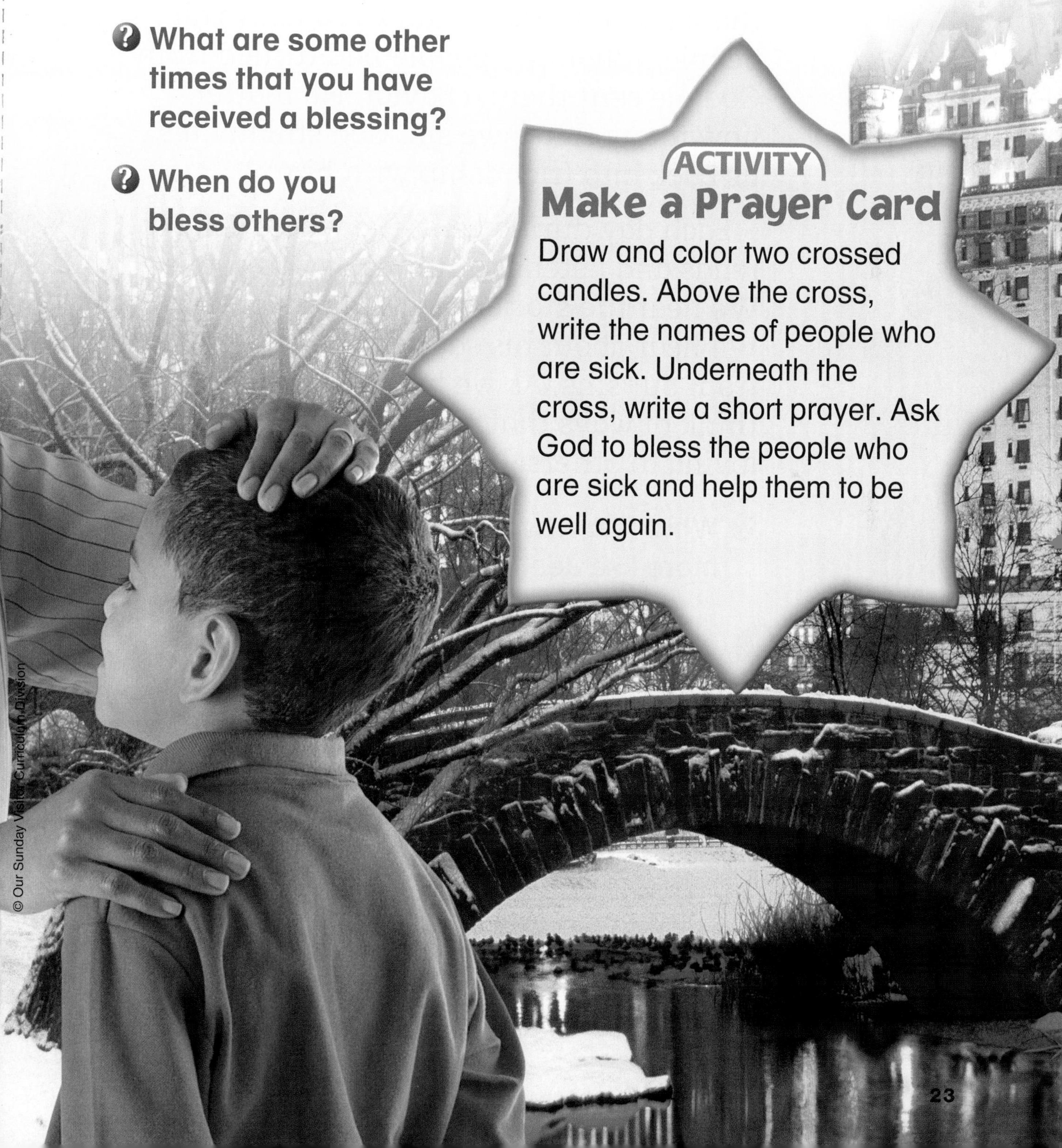

ACTIVITY

Make a Prayer Card

Draw and color two crossed candles. Above the cross, write the names of people who are sick. Underneath the cross, write a short prayer. Ask God to bless the people who are sick and help them to be well again.

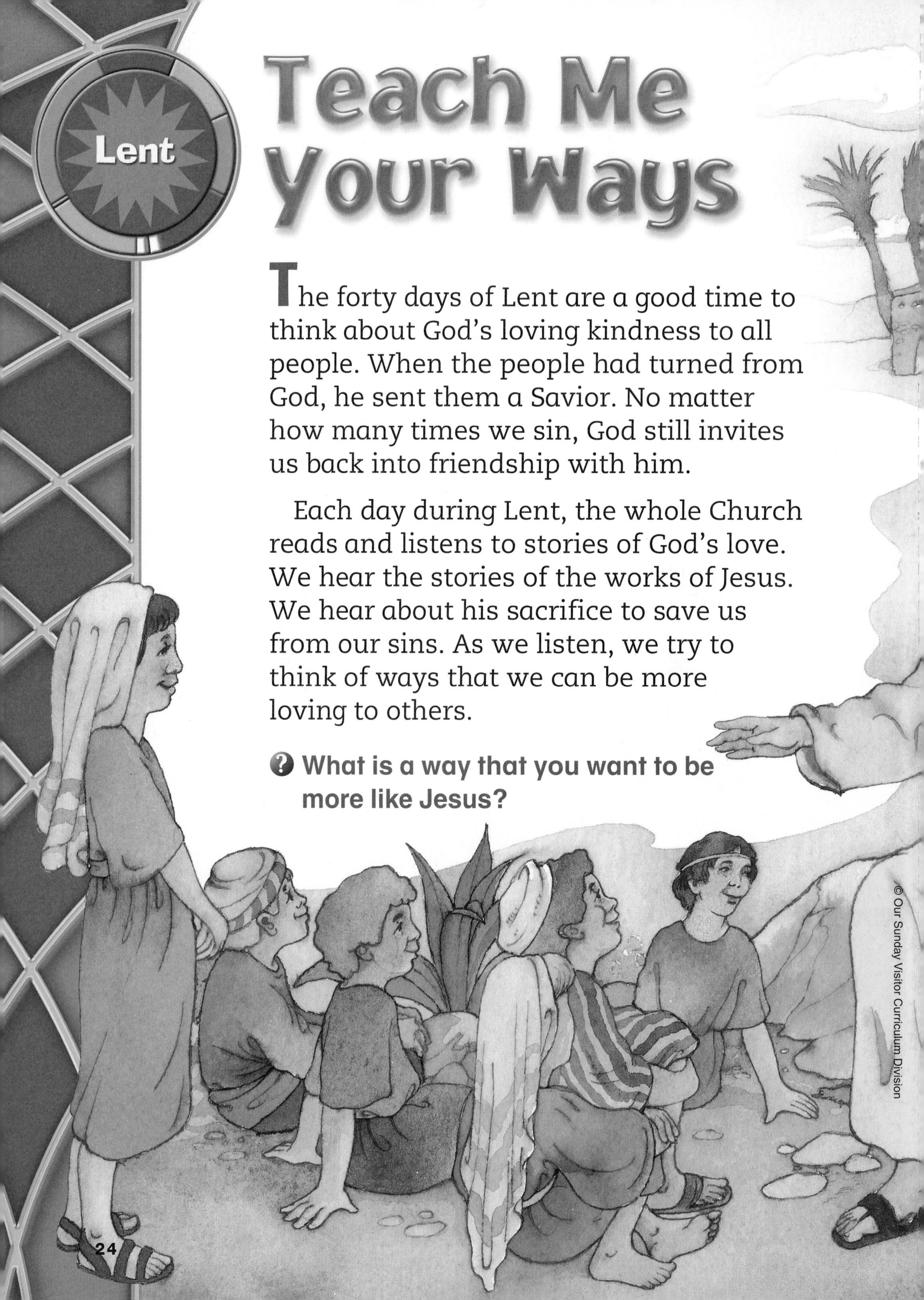

Lent

Teach Me Your Ways

The forty days of Lent are a good time to think about God's loving kindness to all people. When the people had turned from God, he sent them a Savior. No matter how many times we sin, God still invites us back into friendship with him.

Each day during Lent, the whole Church reads and listens to stories of God's love. We hear the stories of the works of Jesus. We hear about his sacrifice to save us from our sins. As we listen, we try to think of ways that we can be more loving to others.

What is a way that you want to be more like Jesus?

Celebrate Lent

Gather

Pray the Sign of the Cross together.

Leader: O Lord open my lips.

All: That my mouth shall praise you.

Leader: Lord Jesus, you have shown us the way to the Father.

All: Lord, have mercy.

Leader: Lord Jesus, you have given us the truth.

All: Christ, have mercy.

Leader: Lord Jesus, you are the Good Shepherd, leading us to everlasting life.

All: Lord, have mercy.

Leader: May almighty God have mercy on us, forgive us our sins, and bring us to everlasting life.

All: Amen.

Listen to God's Word

Leader: A reading from the holy Gospel according to John.

Read John 3:16-17.

The Gospel of the Lord.

All: Praise to you, Lord Jesus Christ.

Signing of the Senses

Sing together the refrain.

Teach me your ways, O Lord.

"Psalm 25: Teach Me Your Ways" ©1969, 1981, and 1997, ICEL

Leader: Let us pray.
Father of our Lord, Jesus Christ, you chose us as your holy people.

All: **Sing the refrain as you trace a cross on your forehead.**

Leader: Jesus shared good news with others.

All: **Sing as you trace a cross on your lips.**

Leader: Jesus, you showed your love by forgiving and healing others.

All: **Sing as you trace a cross on your heart.**

Go Forth!

Leader: Father, your Son Jesus teaches us your ways. Help us to know, love, and serve you, now and forever. In Jesus' name we pray.

All: Amen.

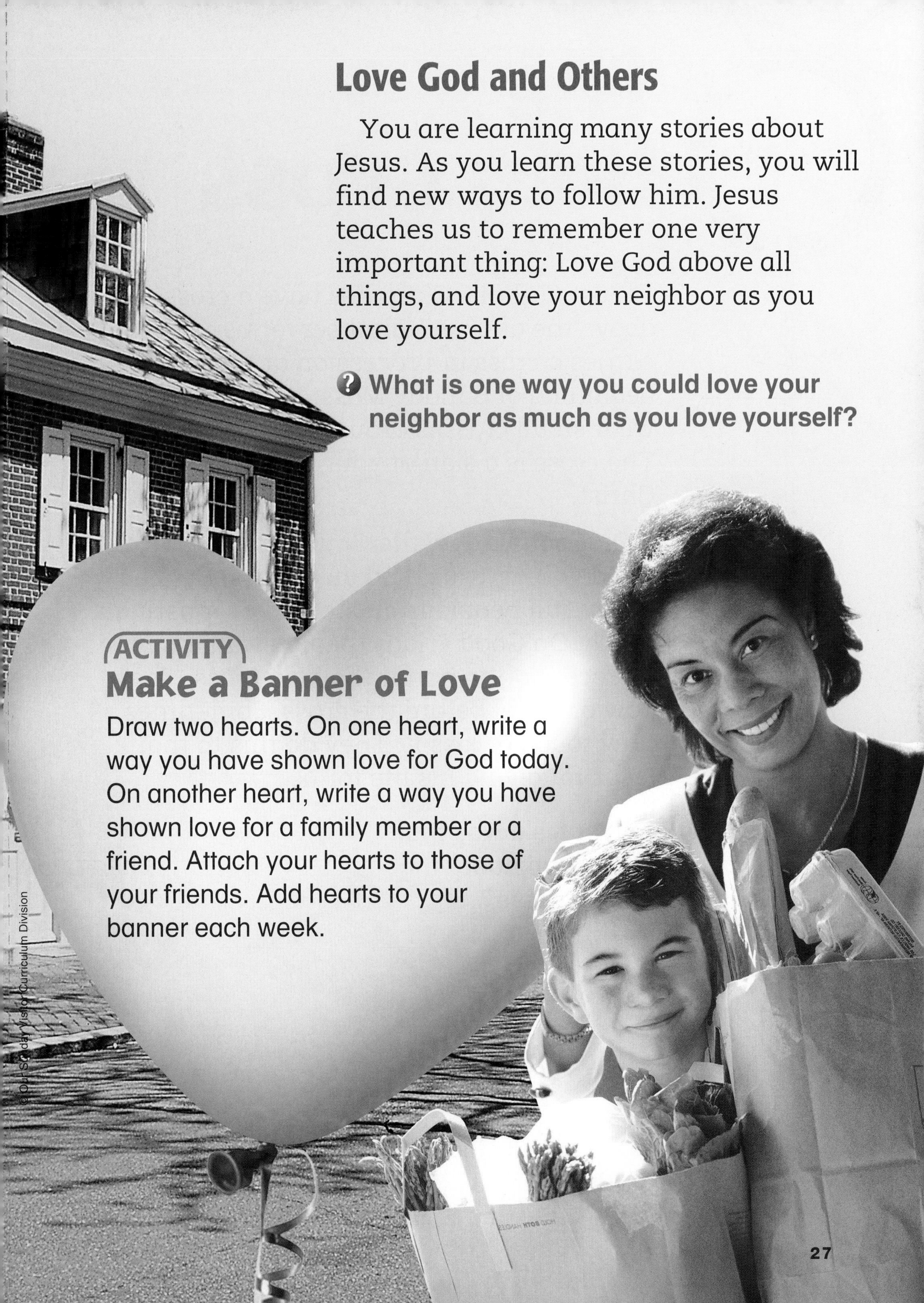

Love God and Others

You are learning many stories about Jesus. As you learn these stories, you will find new ways to follow him. Jesus teaches us to remember one very important thing: Love God above all things, and love your neighbor as you love yourself.

What is one way you could love your neighbor as much as you love yourself?

ACTIVITY

Make a Banner of Love

Draw two hearts. On one heart, write a way you have shown love for God today. On another heart, write a way you have shown love for a family member or a friend. Attach your hearts to those of your friends. Add hearts to your banner each week.

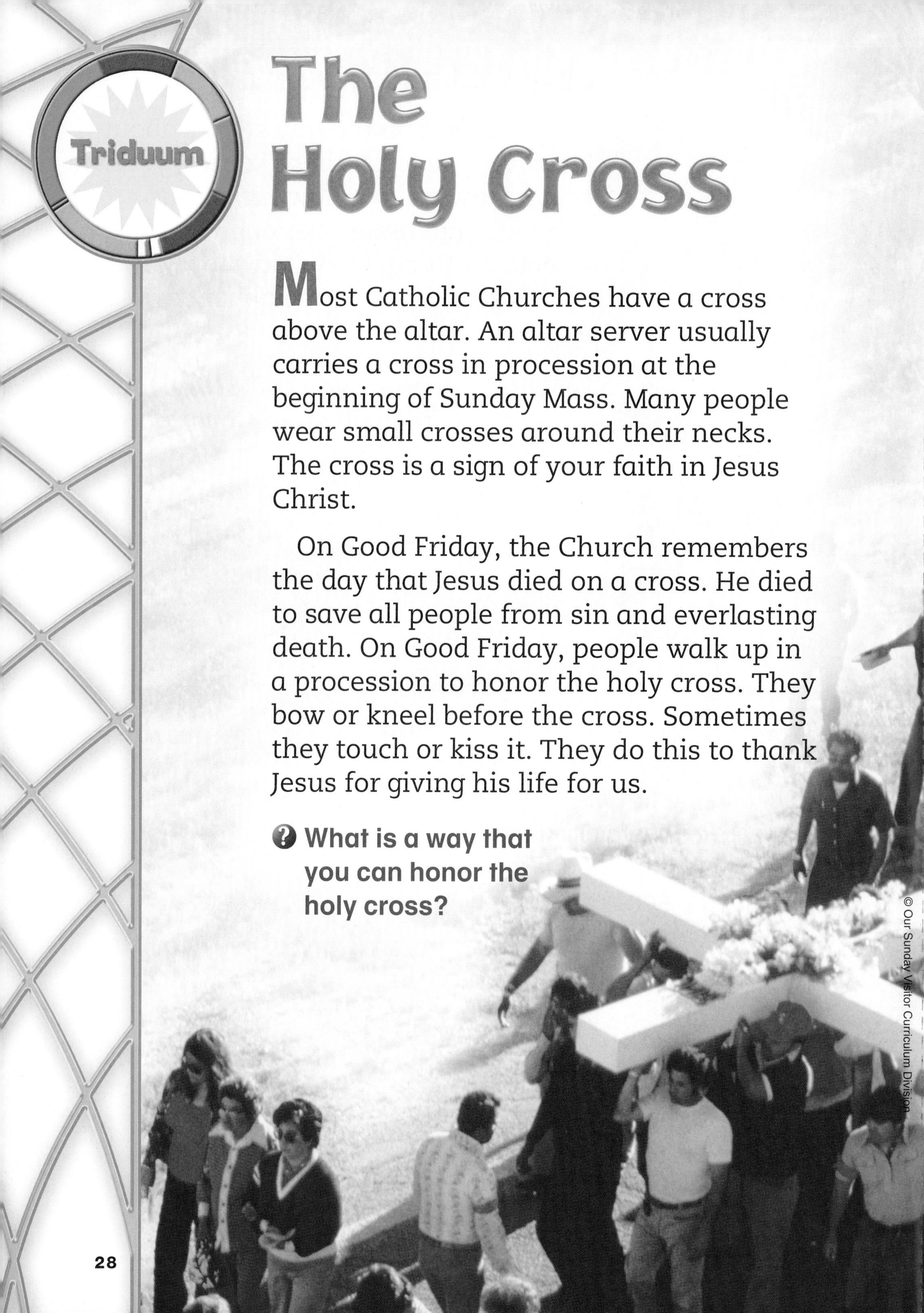

Triduum

The Holy Cross

Most Catholic Churches have a cross above the altar. An altar server usually carries a cross in procession at the beginning of Sunday Mass. Many people wear small crosses around their necks. The cross is a sign of your faith in Jesus Christ.

On Good Friday, the Church remembers the day that Jesus died on a cross. He died to save all people from sin and everlasting death. On Good Friday, people walk up in a procession to honor the holy cross. They bow or kneel before the cross. Sometimes they touch or kiss it. They do this to thank Jesus for giving his life for us.

? What is a way that you can honor the holy cross?

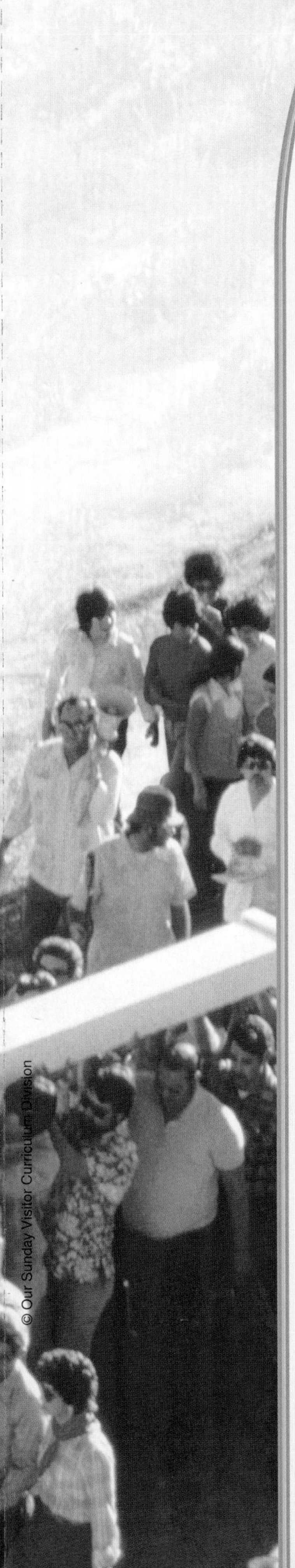

Celebrate the Three Days

Gather

Pray the Sign of the Cross together.

Leader: O Lord, open my lips.

All: That my mouth shall speak your praise.

Leader: Let us pray.

Bow your heads as the leader prays.

All: Amen.

Listen to God's Word

Leader: A reading from the holy Gospel according to Luke.

Read Luke 23:44-49.

The Gospel of the Lord.

All: Praise to you, Lord Jesus Christ.

Prayer of the Faithful

Leader: Let us pray for the holy People of God.

All: Lord, guide your Church.

Leader: Let us pray for our bishop, for all bishops, priests, and deacons, and for all who work in ministry in our Church.

All: Holy Spirit, guide our leaders.

Leader: Let us pray for all in our parish who are preparing for Baptism.

All: Lord, make them members of your family.

Procession to the Cross

Fold your hands and pray silently to Jesus.

Walk up slowly and in silence to honor the cross.

Bow deeply and touch the foot of the cross.

Sing together.

O how good is Christ the Lord!
On the cross he died for me.
In three days he rose again.
Glory be to Jesus! Glory be to Jesus!
Glory be to Jesus!
In three days he rose again.
Glory be to Jesus!

"O How Good is Christ the Lord" Puerto Rican traditional

Go Forth!

Leader: We believe that by his dying
Christ destroyed death forever.
May he give us everlasting life.

All: Amen.

Leader: May almighty God bless us,
the Father, the Son, and the
Holy Spirit.

All: Amen.

Helping Others

Jesus carried his cross to the place where he would die. He loved all people so much he was willing to die for them. When we do something that is difficult in order to help others, sometimes we say that we are "carrying a cross," too. We are willing to think of their needs.

What is something you have done for others, even when it was hard?

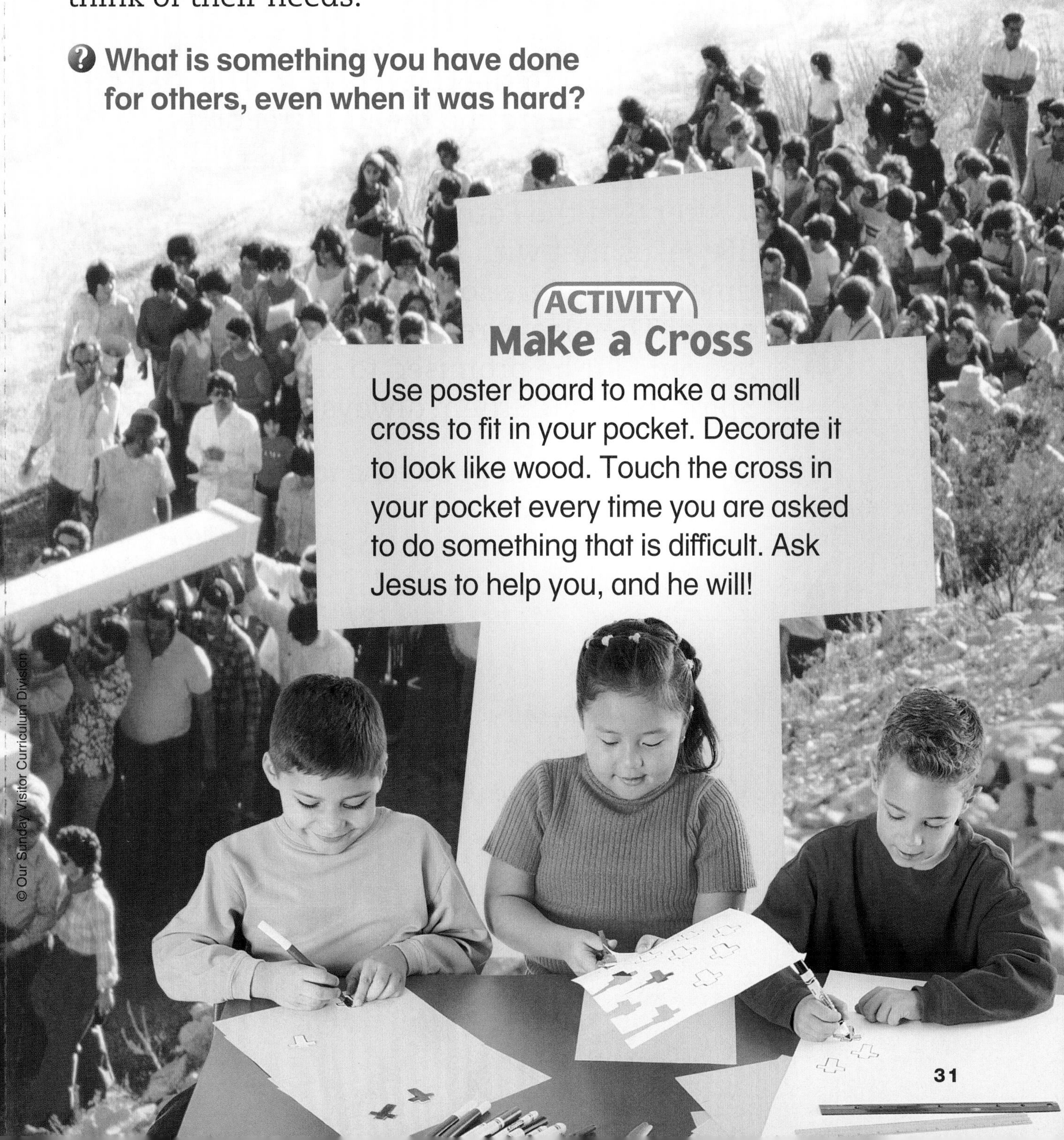

ACTIVITY

Make a Cross

Use poster board to make a small cross to fit in your pocket. Decorate it to look like wood. Touch the cross in your pocket every time you are asked to do something that is difficult. Ask Jesus to help you, and he will!

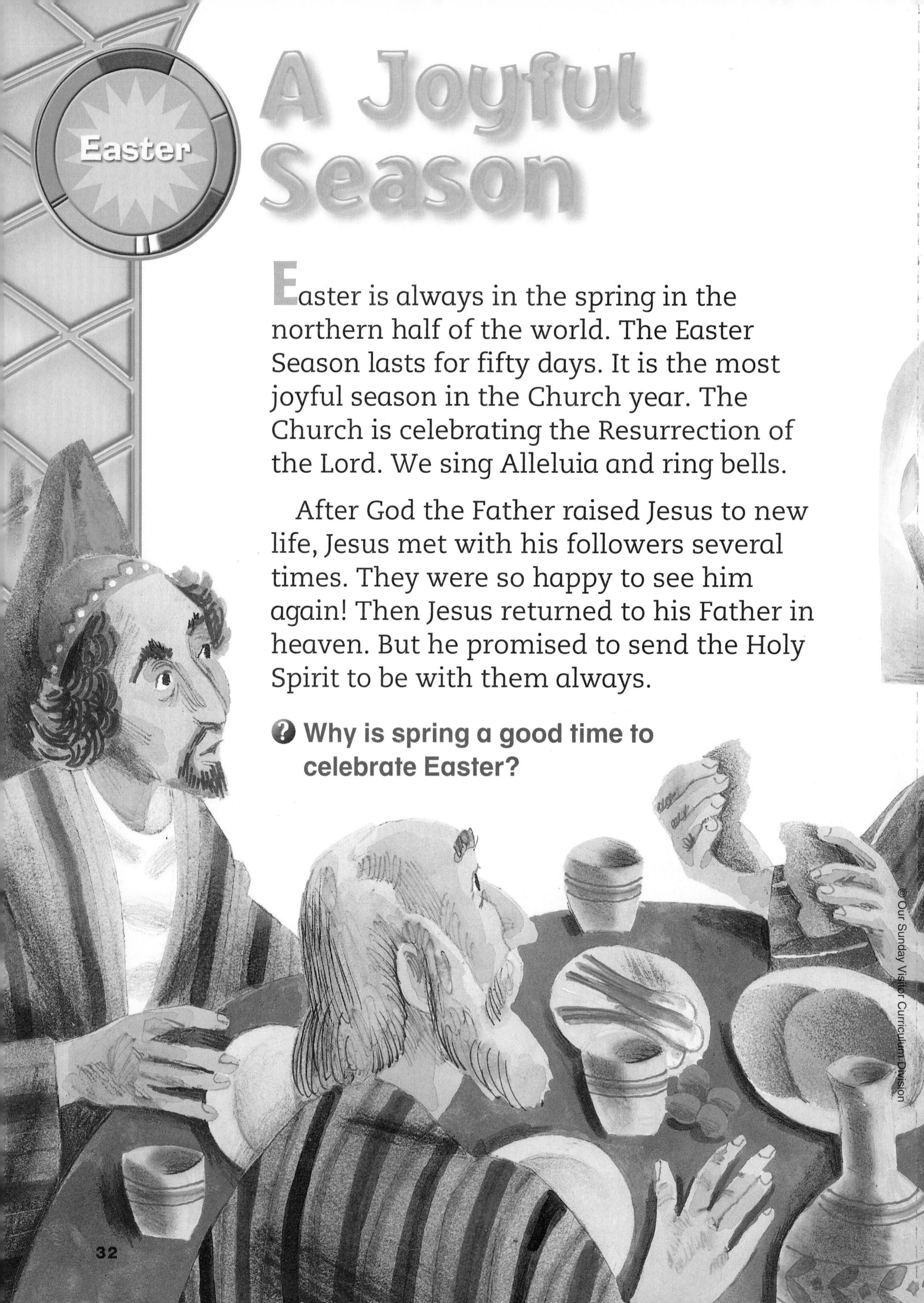

A Joyful Season

Easter is always in the spring in the northern half of the world. The Easter Season lasts for fifty days. It is the most joyful season in the Church year. The Church is celebrating the Resurrection of the Lord. We sing Alleluia and ring bells.

After God the Father raised Jesus to new life, Jesus met with his followers several times. They were so happy to see him again! Then Jesus returned to his Father in heaven. But he promised to send the Holy Spirit to be with them always.

Why is spring a good time to celebrate Easter?

Celebrate Easter

Gather

Pray the Sign of the Cross together.

Leader: Light and peace in Jesus Christ our Lord, alleluia.

All: Thanks be to God, alleluia.

Leader: Let us pray.

Raise your hands as the leader prays.

All: Amen.

Listen to God's Word

Sing together.

¡Aleluya, aleluya! ¡Aleluya, aleluya!
¡Aleluya, aleluya!
¡El Señor resucitó!
¡Aleluya! ¡Aleluya! ¡Aleluya! ¡Aleluya!
¡Aleluya! ¡Aleluya! ¡Aleluya! ¡Aleluya!

"Honduran Alleluia" Honduran traditional

Leader: A reading from the holy Gospel according to Luke.

Read Luke 24:13-35.

The Gospel of the Lord.

All: Praise to you, Lord Jesus Christ. Alleluia, alleluia.

The Lord's Prayer and Sign of Peace

Leader: Let us pray in the words that Jesus taught us.

Raise your hands as you pray.

All: Our Father . . .

Leader: May the God of light and peace fill our hearts and lives.

All: Amen.

Leader: Let us offer to each other a sign of the peace of Christ.

Offer one another a sign of peace.

Go Forth!

Leader: Go in peace, alleluia.

All: Thanks be to God, alleluia.

Good News

The two travelers on the road recognized Jesus when he broke the bread. How surprised they must have been. Jesus was truly alive again! The travelers could not wait to tell others.

What good news can you tell others about Jesus?

ACTIVITY

Make a Card

Make an Easter greeting card to send to a relative. Decorate the front of your card. On the inside, write some good news about Jesus.

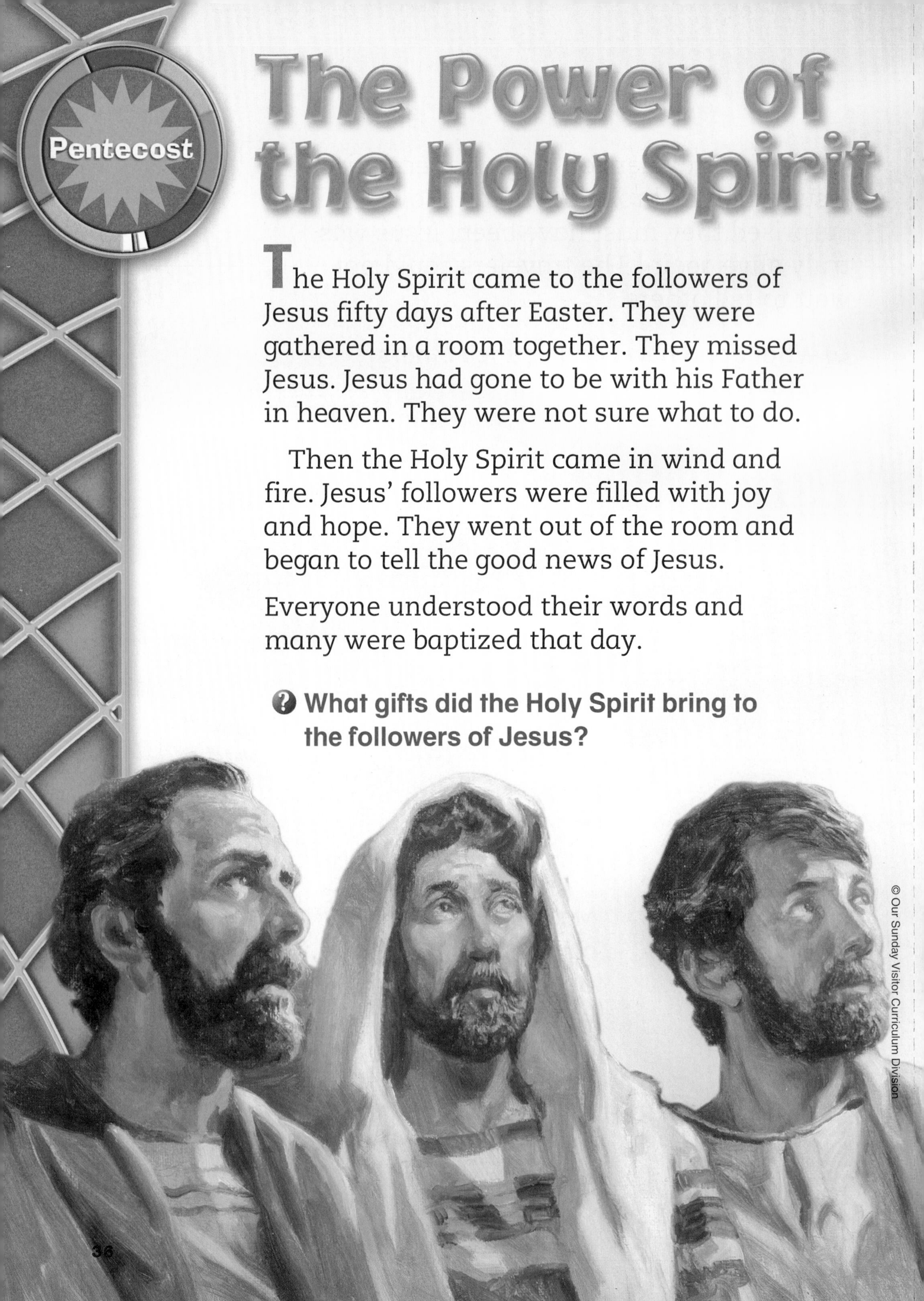

Pentecost

The Power of the Holy Spirit

The Holy Spirit came to the followers of Jesus fifty days after Easter. They were gathered in a room together. They missed Jesus. Jesus had gone to be with his Father in heaven. They were not sure what to do.

Then the Holy Spirit came in wind and fire. Jesus' followers were filled with joy and hope. They went out of the room and began to tell the good news of Jesus.

Everyone understood their words and many were baptized that day.

What gifts did the Holy Spirit bring to the followers of Jesus?

Gather

Pray the Sign of the Cross together.

Leader: Light and peace in Jesus Christ our Lord, Alleluia.

All: Thanks be to God, Alleluia.

Leader: Let us pray.

Raise your hands as the leader prays.

All: Amen.

Listen to God's Word

Leader: A reading from the Letter of Paul to the Romans.

Read Romans 8:26–27.

The word of the Lord.

All: Thanks be to God.

Sing together.

God sends us his Spirit to befriend
and help us.
Recreate and guide us, Spirit-Friend
Spirit who enlivens, sanctifies,
enlightens,
Sets us free, is now our Spirit-Friend.
Spirit of our Maker, Spirit-Friend.

Go Forth!

Final Blessing

Bow your heads as the leader prays.

Leader: May the Lord bless us and keep us.

All: Amen.

Leader: May the Lord's face shine upon us.

All: Amen.

Leader: May the Lord look upon us with kindness, and give us peace.

All: Thanks be to God,
Alleluia, Alleluia.

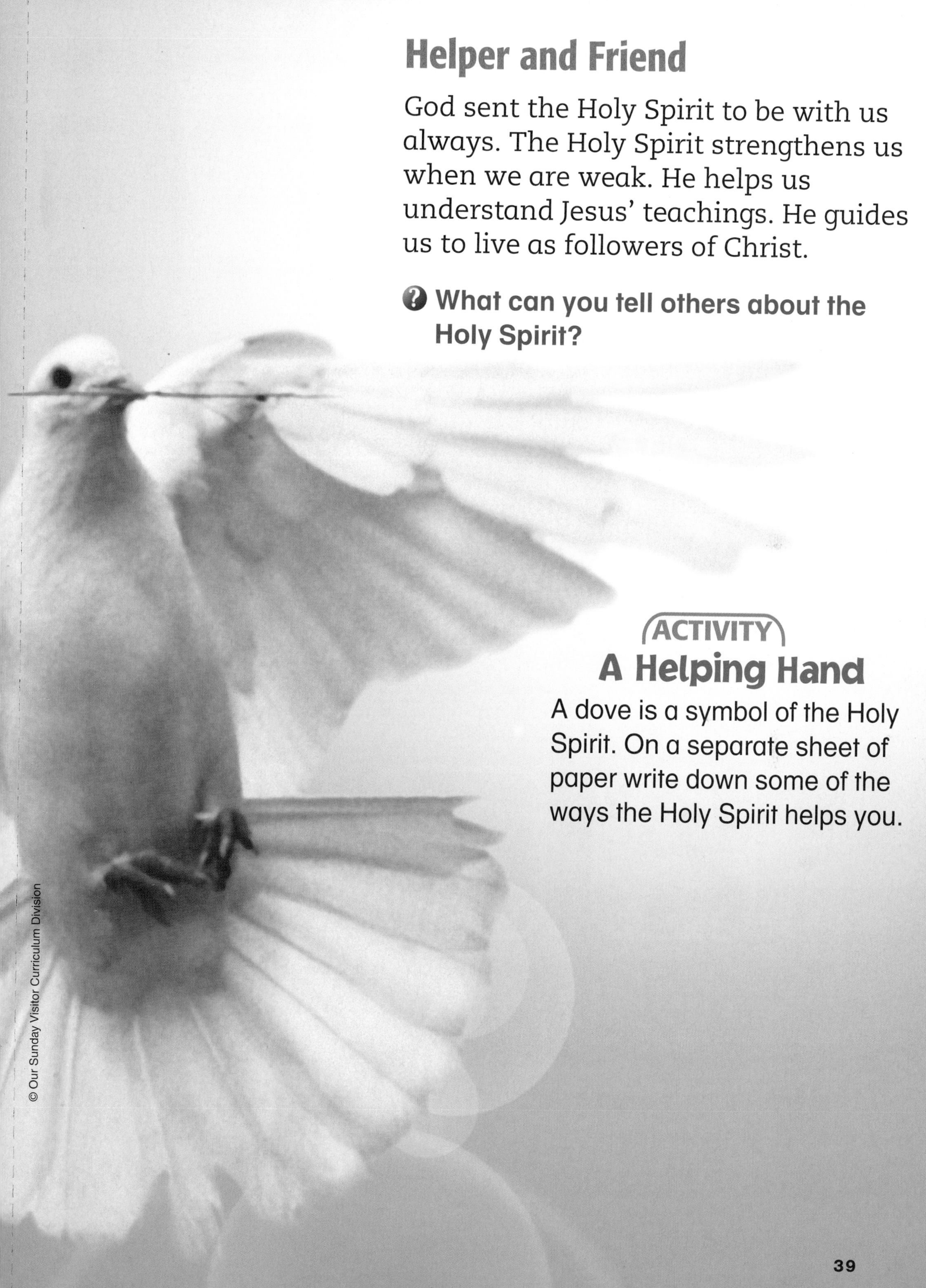

Helper and Friend

God sent the Holy Spirit to be with us always. The Holy Spirit strengthens us when we are weak. He helps us understand Jesus' teachings. He guides us to live as followers of Christ.

What can you tell others about the Holy Spirit?

ACTIVITY

A Helping Hand

A dove is a symbol of the Holy Spirit. On a separate sheet of paper write down some of the ways the Holy Spirit helps you.

Unit 1 Revelation

In this unit you will...

learn that God gave us many gifts. God's gifts tell us about what he is like. We can learn about God's gifts and his love from the Bible. Adam and Eve turned away from God. God kept loving them anyway. Jesus, God's only Son, is his greatest gift. Jesus is our Savior. He brings us back into friendship with God, his Father.

Faith in Action!

Catholic Social Teaching Principle: Care for God's Creation

DISCOVER

Catholic Social Teaching:

Care for God's Creation

Faith in Action!

CATHOLIC SOCIAL TEACHING

In this unit you learned that God made everything. God created the earth, the ocean, and the sun. He made animals and insects. God made you, too. God gave people the special job of taking care of all that he made.

Care for Creation

God calls you to protect his gifts and to use them wisely. You show God respect when you take care of the planet and all that is in it.

God wants people to have the water, the food, and the air they need to live. The things people do today can help save God's gifts for people to use many years from now.

? What are some ways you can care for God's creation?

Helping water the plants

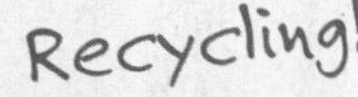

Recycling!

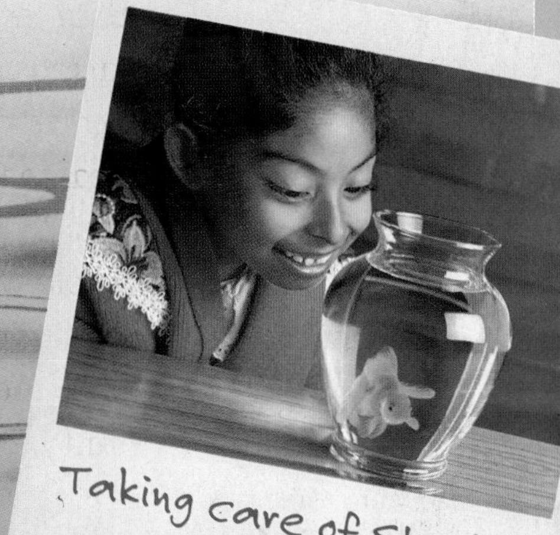

Taking care of Stanley

CONNECT

With the Call to Justice

Adopt a Lake

Everything needs water to live and grow. Let's look at what one community did to care for God's special gift of water.

Children in a school in Lakeland, Florida, found their own way to care for creation. The Catholic school children worked with their community to clean up a lake. Their program was called Adopt a Lake.

Families spent a Saturday cleaning up a lake. They picked up trash. They removed harmful plants. They put signs up to remind people to care for the lake. These children showed how important it is to care for God's special gift of water.

? How did the children take care of God's creation?

Reach Out!

Plan a Garden

Now it is your turn. You know that G d asks you to care for creation. Imagine that you re planting a garden. Work with a partner to make ur plans. Use a separate sheet of paper to write d vn your plans.

1. List three things you would like to grow.
2. List things you need for the garden.
3. What does the garden need to keep growing?
4. How would you share your garden?

Make a Difference

Clean a Playground Work together as a class to clean up the school playground. Then talk to first-grade classes about why you cleaned the playground. Invite other classes to find a way to care for God's creation at your school.

Unit 1 Review

A **Work with Words** Complete each sentence with the correct word from the Word Bank.

WORD BANK
Bible
Jesus
savior
God
Creation

1. The Old and New Testaments make up the ________________.
2. You are made in the image and likeness of ________________.
3. God promised to send a ________________.
4. God's greatest gift is ________________.
5. ________________ is all that God made.

Circle the correct answer.

6. Who told the story of the Good Shepherd?

   David **John** **Jesus**

7. What is God's word written by humans?

   a book **the Bible** **God**

8. Who wrote the psalms?

   David **Mary** **Jesus**

9. Which part of the Bible is about Jesus?

   New Testament **Psalms** **Old Testament**

10. Who guided the Bible writers?

    humans **Adam** **God**

B **Check Understanding** Draw a line from Column A to the best ending in Column B.

Column A	Column B
11. Humans are	**a.** everything that is good.
12. God is the Creator of	**b.** your choices.
13. You are responsible for	**c.** the most special part of God's creation.
14. You can learn about God by	**d.** all people.
15. Jesus cared for	**e.** reading the Bible.

C **Make Connections** Use the words in the Word Bank to solve the puzzle.

WORD BANK

sin
original sin
Son of God
Old Testament
New Testament

19. 16. 17. 20. 18.

Across

16. The sin committed by the first people

17. The name of Jesus that tells you that God is his Father

18. Choosing to disobey God

Down

19. Tells about the life and teachings of Jesus and the early Church

20. Tells about God and his people before Jesus was born

Unit 2 Trinity

In this unit you will...

learn about each Person of the Holy Trinity. God the Father loves and cares for us as a faithful parent. We can trust and rely on God the Father. Jesus, the Son of God, sets an example for us with his life and teachings. God the Holy Spirit guides the Church and helps us to be holy.

Faith in Action!

Catholic Social Teaching Principle:
Life and Dignity of the Human Person

DISCOVER

Catholic Social Teaching:

Life and Dignity of the Human Person

In this unit you learned that God cares for you as his own child. Jesus, the Son of God, shows us how to love God and love others. The Holy Spirit is with us, helping us follow the law of love.

Respect Each Person

God created you in his own image. There is no one else exactly like you. God blessed you with many gifts and talents. God did this for everyone!

Sometimes it is easy to forget this good news. You think of the things you can't do, or the things you don't like about someone else. God calls you to treat all people, yourself included, with respect. You are wonderfully made!

How can you show respect for yourself?

How can you show respect for others?

CONNECT

With the Call to Justice

Wonderfully Made

Every person deserves respect. Let's look at how some special children are learning that they are wonderfully made.

Jason cannot do math. Megan cannot walk or talk. Danny can't sit up.

These children, and others like them who have special needs, live at St. Joseph's Center in Pennsylvania. The people who work at St. Joseph's can give these children the care they need. The staff of St. Joseph's Center helps the children see themselves with God's eyes. They remind the children that they are wonderfully made. The workers at St. Joseph's and the children's families see with God's eyes. They do not worry about what the children can't do. They see only what the children can do.

Jason can give the best hugs. Megan smiles at everyone. Danny tells everyone he loves them.

How do you think the children at St. Joseph's Center feel about themselves?

Reach Out!

Write a Letter

Now it is your turn to help someone see that he or she is wonderfully made. Think of someone you know who needs to hear this good news. Use a separate sheet of paper to write this person a letter. In your letter, follow these steps.

1. Tell the person why you care for him or her.
2. Name some of the gifts and talents that make the person special.
3. Tell the person that he or she is wonderfully made in God's image.

Make a Difference

Collect Toys or Blankets Work together as a class to collect new stuffed toys or blankets, or used ones in good condition. Share the toys or blankets with children in a local hospital or homeless shelter. Talk to a first-grade class about your project. Invite other classes to find ways to show respect for all people.

Unit 2 Review

A **Work with Words** Complete each sentence with the letter of the correct word or words from the Word Bank.

1. People who follow Jesus are called ________.
2. Jesus promised to send the ________.
3. Listening and talking to God is called ________.
4. Jesus taught us to call God ________.
5. The three Persons in one God is called the ________.

WORD BANK

a. Holy Spirit
b. disciples
c. Holy Trinity
d. Father
e. prayer

B **Check Understanding** Complete each sentence in Column 1 with the letter of the correct word or words from Column 2.

Column 1	Column 2
6. The third Person of the Holy Trinity is the ________.	a. Mary
7. The Mother of God's Son is ________.	b. John Bosco
8. The first Person of the Holy Trinity is the ________.	c. Holy Spirit
9. A saint who helped homeless boys is ________.	d. Jesus
10. The second Person of the Holy Trinity is ________.	e. Father

Circle the correct answer.

11. You can always ________ God to love you.

respect **trust** **know**

12. After Jesus was _______, he traveled all over the country where he lived.

baptized **older** **risen**

13. Jesus teaches today through the _______.

Church **town** **disciples**

14. You can follow Jesus by _______ people.

mistreating **forgetting** **forgiving**

15. A _______ of Jesus follows his example.

enemy **saint** **disciple**

C Make Connections Complete each sentence below.

16. A saint is a holy person who

____.

17. Prayer is talking to and

____.

18. To trust is to believe in and

____.

19. The Temple was the holy building in Jerusalem where

____.

20. Disciples are people who choose

____.

Unit 3 Jesus Christ

In this unit you will...

learn that God teaches us to love as he loved. God gave his people the Ten Commandments. Jesus gave us a new commandment of love. We show love by doing good. Our conscience is a gift God gives that helps us know right from wrong. Jesus teaches us that God our Father always offers forgiveness and shows us mercy.

Faith in Action!

Catholic Social Teaching Principle:
Rights and Responsibilities of the Human Person

DISCOVER

Catholic Social Teaching:

Rights and Responsibilities of the Human Person

In this unit you learned that all people are your neighbors. Jesus teaches you to love your neighbors. You can show love in many ways.

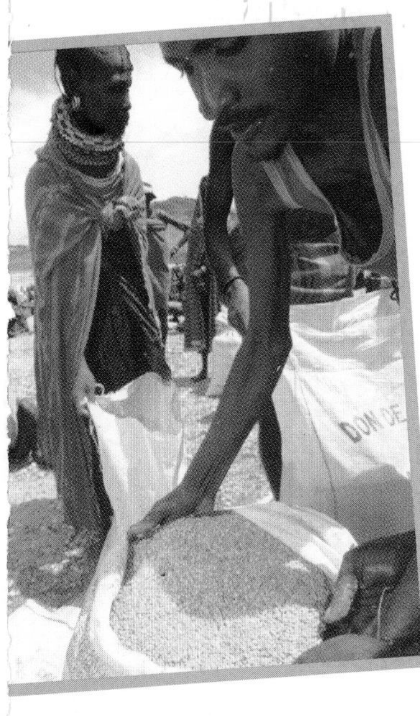

Rights and Responsibilities

Humans need many things to live happy and healthy lives. Some of these things are:

- a safe place to live.
- healthful food and clean water.
- health care.

These important things are called **human rights**. All people deserve to have these needs met.

The Church teaches that humans have rights because they are made in God's image. Each person has the responsibility to make sure other people get what they need. We are called to protect the human rights of all people.

What are some ways that people can make sure others get what they need?

CONNECT

With the Call to Justice

Peter Takes Responsibility

Sometimes people's rights are not protected. Let's look at how one holy man took responsibility for helping others.

Peter Claver was born in Spain, hundreds of years ago. He became a priest. Peter felt called by God to travel halfway around the world to South America. He wanted to share God's love with the people of Colombia.

When Peter got off the ship in the port of Cartagena, he saw a terrible sight. Men, women, and children from Africa had been taken from their homes to be sold as slaves. They were hungry, sick, and frightened.

Peter spent the next forty years caring for these people. He helped them get food and clothing. He cared for them when they were sick. Peter could not end slavery, but he took responsibility for doing what he could to help. He became known as "the slave of the slaves." Today we call him Saint Peter Claver.

? How did Saint Peter Claver show that he believed all people have rights?

• Watch out for younger children on the playground.
• Make sure your pet has food and clean water everyday.

Reach Out!

SERVE
Your Community

Make a List

Saint Peter Claver did his best to help those who were harmed by slavery. At your age, you cannot do much to change the world. Right now, you can do things to make people happier and healthier, close to where you live.

On a separate sheet of paper, make a list of ways you can be responsible at home and at school. Think of things that will help others. Here are some ideas to get you started.

- Watch out for younger children on the playground.
- Make sure your pet has food and clean water every day.

Make a Difference

Make New Friends With your teacher's help, learn more about children in another school, town, state, or country. Exchange class letters or e-mail. Tell the other children about your neighborhood and your school. Ask the other children to tell you about their lives.

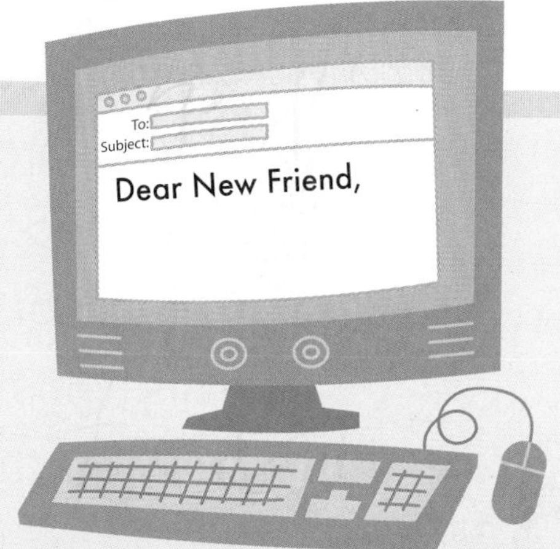

Unit 3 Review

A Work with Words Use the clues to find the words in the word search. Circle each word when you find it.

c	o	m	m	a	n	d	m	e	n	t	s
o	a	e	e	c	p	r	z	o	s	t	m
n	f	s	r	c	z	s	l	J	p	r	o
s	a	b	c	i	o	p	o	e	a	b	r
c	q	n	y	d	d	z	v	s	q	c	t
i	w	g	t	e	h	r	e	u	m	o	a
e	f	r	g	n	v	z	a	s	y	h	l
n	z	s	m	t	a	o	b	e	d	c	a
c	p	i	e	f	c	v	e	n	i	a	l
e	x	n	y	f	o	r	g	i	v	e	s

1. God's laws
2. The free choice to disobey God
3. What God does if you are sorry
4. Sin that does not completely remove you from God's grace
5. Very serious sin
6. Loving forgiveness and kindness
7. Jesus teaches us to do this
8. This is not a sin
9. This helps you to know right from wrong
10. He gave the law of love

B **Check Understanding** Draw a line from each item in Column A to match the correct ending in Column B.

Column A	Column B
11. Jesus teaches that all people are	**a.** the way you want to be treated.
12. The Great Commandment tells you to treat others	**b.** is in need.
13. Jesus' law of love says, "Love one another as	**c.** your neighbors.
14. A neighbor can be someone who helps or	**d.** the gift God gave you to help you make good choices.
15. Your conscience is	**e.** I have loved you."
16. To make a good choice, you must	**f.** asks you to forgive.
17. When someone has been unkind or unfair, Jesus	**g.** do all you can to help make up for the wrong you did.
18. To ask forgiveness, you should	**h.** listen to your conscience.
19. To help you make better choices, you can always	**i.** pray.

C **Make Connections** Write your answer on the lines.

20. Angela pushed ahead of you in line in the cafeteria. How can you show that you are a follower of Jesus?

Unit 4 The Church

In this unit you will...

learn that God shares his life with the Church. Grace is sharing in God's life. The sacraments are signs and celebrations of God's life. They give us grace. They help us celebrate our friendship with Jesus. They help us follow Jesus. The Church year celebrates the life, death and Resurrection of Jesus.

Faith in Action!

Catholic Social Teaching Principle: Dignity of Work and Rights of Workers

Chapter 10 Signs of Love

Let Us Pray

Leader: God, thank you for sharing your life with us.
"Come and see the works of God,
awesome in the deeds done for us."
Psalm 66:5

All: God, thank you for sharing your life with us.
Amen.

Activity Let's Begin

My Abuela and Me Some weekends I visit my grandmother. I call her *Abuela*. She meets me after school on Friday and gives me a big hug. Then we take the subway to her apartment.

Abuela makes my favorite foods and plays games with me. She listens to me and takes care of me. Sometimes Abuela leaves me a note in my book bag. This is another sign of her love for me.

- What are the signs of love in this story?

That the grandmaw gives a note.

Show Love As a class, think of as many signs of love as you can. Then write down three signs of love you share in your family.

Jesus Shares Life

Focus What are the sacraments?

Faith Fact

People of any age can be baptized.

Jesus' actions were signs of love that brought people closer to God. Jesus welcomed people who felt alone. He fed people who were hungry. Jesus forgave and healed people. In these ways Jesus shared God's life with others.

Jesus asked his disciples to continue sharing his love. The Holy Spirit gave the disciples the power to do what Jesus had done.

SCRIPTURE Acts 8:4–12

People Everywhere Believe

Philip traveled to different towns to tell others the good news about Jesus. He shared Jesus' message and love and even healed people who were sick. Many people began to believe in Jesus and were baptized.

Based on Acts 8:4–12

Why did the people ask to be baptized?

Holy Signs

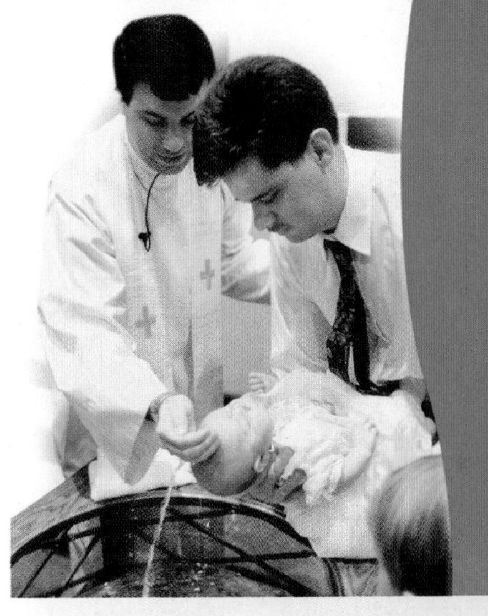

The Catholic Church shares God's life and love through special celebrations called sacraments. A **sacrament** is a holy sign that comes from Jesus and gives God's life. This sharing in God's life is called **grace**.

Baptism is the first sacrament a person receives. Through Baptism a person is given new life in Christ. He or she becomes a child of God and member of the Church.

In the celebration of Baptism, a priest or deacon pours water over the head of the person being baptized and says, "I baptize you in the name of the Father, and of the Son, and of the Holy Spirit." The person receives a lit candle as a sign of walking in the light of Jesus.

Words of Faith

A **sacrament** is a holy sign that comes from Jesus and gives life.

Grace is sharing in God's life.

What do you know about your own Baptism?

Activity **Share Your Faith**

Think: What are some ways you can walk in the light of Jesus?

Share: Share your thoughts with a small group.

Act: Write one thing you will do to follow Jesus this week.

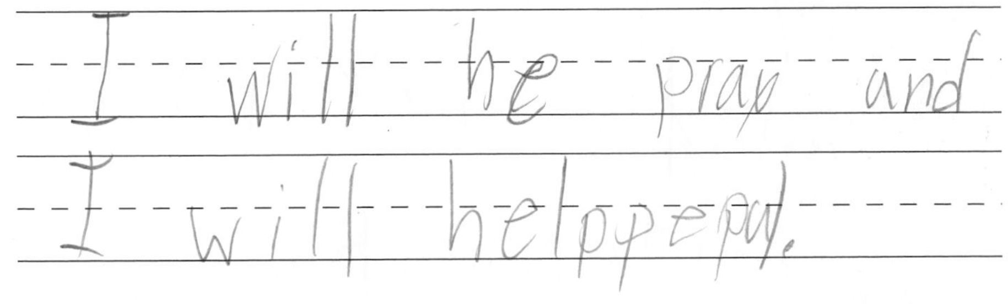

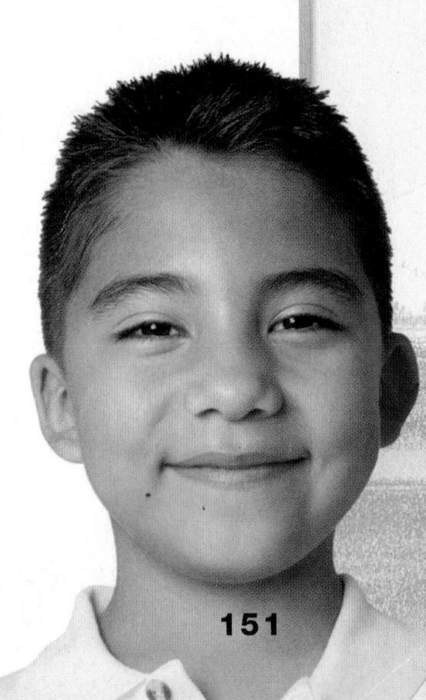

The Seven Sacraments

Focus **How do people become members of the Church?**

Baptism

The sacraments give new life, healing, nourishment, and a share in the work of Jesus. There are seven sacraments.

The sacraments celebrate Jesus' presence among his people. When you receive the sacraments, you grow in your love for God and others. God's life in you grows stronger.

Confirmation

What sacraments have you seen celebrated?

What sacraments will you receive soon?

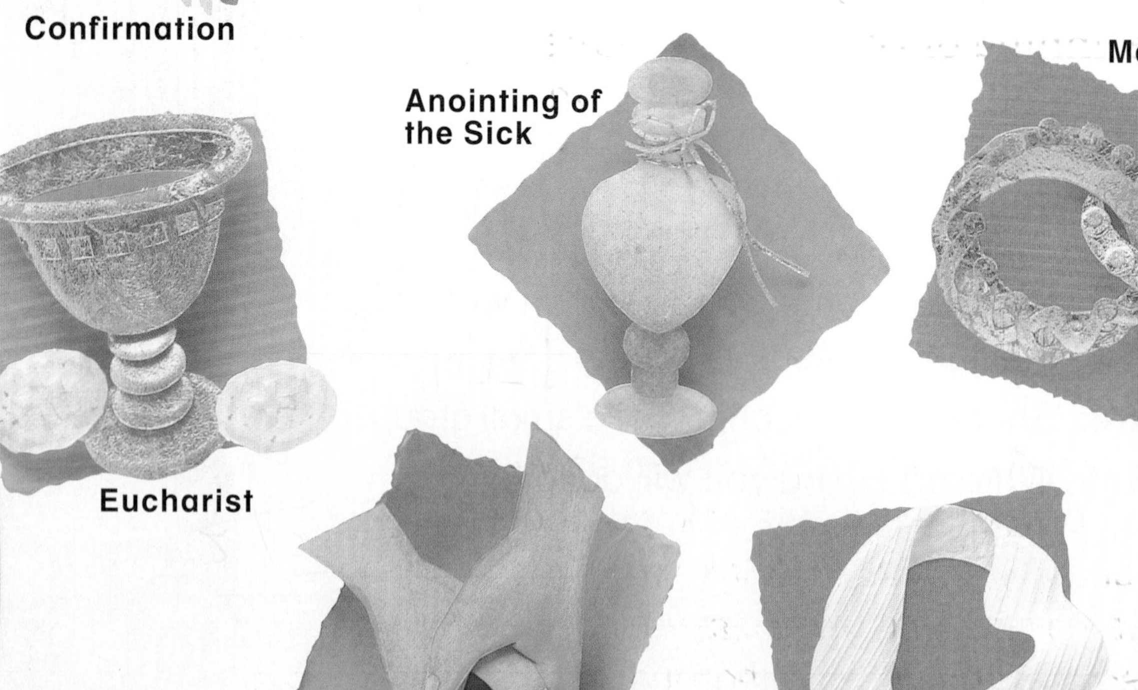

Anointing of the Sick

Matrimony

Eucharist

Reconciliation

Holy Orders

The Sacraments of Initiation

Baptism, Confirmation, and Eucharist are the Sacraments of Initiation. *Initiation* means "beginning." These sacraments welcome new members into the Church.

Through Baptism a person is given new life in Christ. In Confirmation the Holy Spirit strengthens people to be followers of Jesus. In the Eucharist, Jesus' Body and Blood are received.

People of any age can become members of the Catholic Church. Sometimes all three Sacraments of Initiation are received in the same celebration. This happens at the beginning of Easter. Other times the Sacraments are spread out over many years. Everyone is invited to follow Jesus and join the Church.

Activity Connect Your Faith

Welcome New Members What do you think new Catholics need to know about Christ and the Church? Make a welcome card and bring it to your parish for someone who has just become a Catholic.

Welcome

Celebrations

How are the sacraments signs for the Church?

Each of the sacraments is a sign and a celebration of God's love. In the sacraments you receive grace. God's own love and life make you more loving. The grace of the sacraments helps each follower of Jesus. It helps the whole Church community, too.

Sacrament	What It Celebrates	How It Helps the Church
Baptism	Becoming children of God and members of the Church	Welcomes new members into the Christian family
Confirmation	Being strengthened with the gift of the Holy Spirit	Gives members the strength to follow Jesus' example
Eucharist	Sharing the Body and Blood of Jesus	Feeds, heals, and unites the members of the Body of Christ
Reconciliation	God's forgiveness when we are sorry for sin	Brings people back into the Church and helps make peace
Anointing of the Sick	God's healing love	Gives support to people who are elderly or ill
Matrimony	The lifelong love of a man and a woman who become a new family	Builds family love and gives an example of loving care
Holy Orders	The call to serve God as a deacon, priest, or bishop	Strengthens men to be leaders and to serve the Church

How do the Sacraments help the Church?

Activity

Live Your Faith

Write About Sacraments Write about how the sacraments are signs of God's love. Use each of the letters in the word GRACE.

G od

R is in

A gen and

C ela brated

E nter nal life

Prayer for Gathering

Gather and begin with the Sign of the Cross.

Leader: Blessed be the name of the Lord.

All: Now and forever.

Reader: A reading from the First Letter of Paul to the Corinthians.

Read 1 Corinthians 12:12.

The word of the Lord.

All: Thanks be to God.

Leader: Let us pray.

Bow your heads as the leader prays.

All: Amen.

Sing together the refrain.

We come to share our story,
we come to break the bread.
We come to know our rising
from the dead.

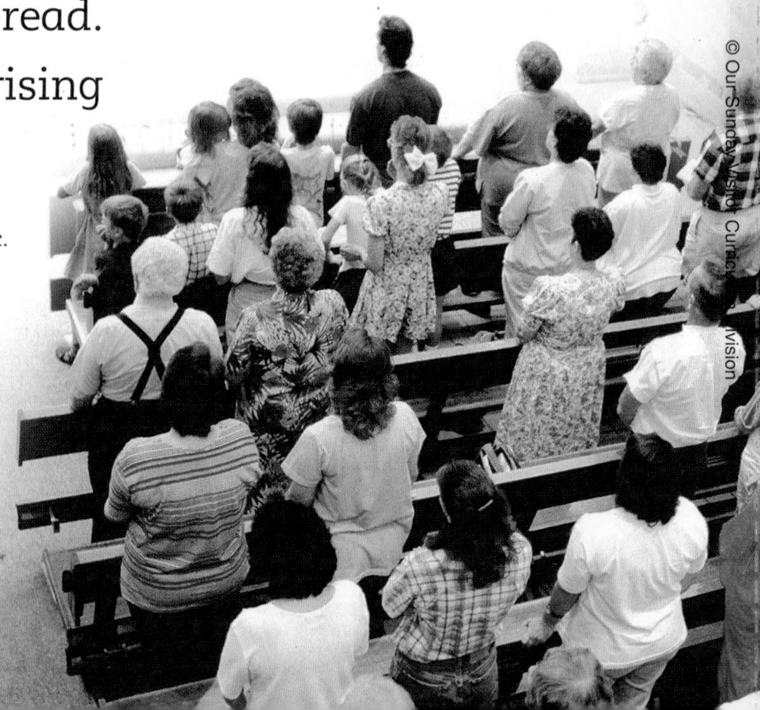

Review

A **Work with Words** Write the letter of the correct words from the Word Bank to complete each sentence.

WORD BANK

a. sacrament
b. Holy Spirit
c. candle
d. love
e. grace
f. Initiation

1. Baptism and Eucharist are sacraments of ______.
2. At Baptism, a ______ is given to show the light of Jesus.
3. In Confirmation, you are made stronger by the ______.
4. A ______ is a holy sign that comes from Jesus.
5. Sharing in God's life is called ______.
6. Each sacrament is a sign of God's ______.

B **Check Understanding** Circle **T** if the sentence is TRUE. Circle **F** if the sentence is FALSE.

7. God's own love and life that make you more loving is called community.

   T **F**

8. God's grace helps the whole Church community.

   T **F**

9. Eucharist is one of the seven sacraments.

   T **F**

10. Name one thing that happens in Baptism.

    ____

    ____

Family Faith

Catholics Believe

- Grace is sharing in God's life.
- Sacraments are holy signs that come from Jesus and give grace.

SCRIPTURE

Read Mark 14:22–25 about the first Eucharist at the Last Supper.

GO online **www.osvcurriculum.com**
For weekly scripture readings and seasonal resources

Activity

Live Your Faith

Look Back Discuss the Sacraments of Initiation. Recall these special days with your children by sharing pictures and videos. Talk about how your family celebrates special days. Have family members choose favorite photos and stories to include in a scrapbook about one sacrament.

▲ Saint John Berchmans, 1599–1621

People of Faith

John was a prayerful, friendly and cheerful person. He was about to become a priest when he died suddenly. John was known for his love of prayer and his work as an altar boy. When he was only 7, he would sometimes serve at 2 or 3 masses a day. People remembered how prayerful John was and how he loved the celebration of Eucharist. For this reason, John was named the patron saint of altar servers. His feast day is August 13.

Family Prayer

Saint John, pray for us that we may always show respect and joy as we celebrate the sacraments. Amen.

In Unit 4 your child is learning about the CHURCH.

 CCC *See Catechism of the Catholic Church 1145–1152 for further reading on chapter content.*

Chapter 11 The Church and Forgiveness

Invite

Leader: Thank you, God, for your forgiveness.
"Lord, you are kind and forgiving,
most loving to all who call on you."
Psalm 86:5

All: Thank you, God, for your forgiveness. Amen.

Activity Let's Begin

New Again Jared has a little brother named Benny. Benny has a special teddy bear named Fuzzy. Benny loved Fuzzy so much that all its fuzz came off. One of Fuzzy's legs tore open, and its stuffing began to fall out.

Jared went to his aunt for help. Benny stood by and watched her sew up Fuzzy. Soon Fuzzy was as good as it could be. Benny was as happy as he could be, too.

- Why was Benny happy?

Becaus Fussy

Share a Story Tell another story about something broken that was fixed or something lost that was found.

Explore

Repairing Hurts

How can you show you are sorry and ask for forgiveness?

Benny's aunt fixed Fuzzy's torn leg. How do you fix the hurts that you cause? In this story, Jesus shows you how.

SCRIPTURE Luke 7:36–39, 48–50

The Woman Who Was Sorry

One day, Jesus was having dinner. An uninvited woman came into the room. The woman knelt at the feet of Jesus. She was sorry for her sins. Her tears fell on Jesus' feet. Then she dried his feet with her long hair. After that she poured sweet-smelling oil on his feet.

Jesus spoke up for the woman. "She has bathed [my feet] with her tears and . . . anointed my feet with ointment. So I tell you, her many sins have been forgiven; hence, she has shown great love."

Then Jesus said to the woman, "Your sins are forgiven . . . Your faith has saved you; go in peace."

Based on Luke 7:36–39, 48–50

How did the woman show she was sorry for her sins?

How do you show you are sorry?

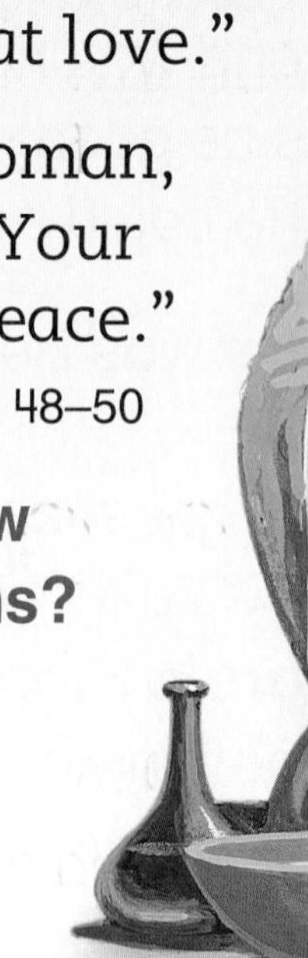

Examination of Conscience

There are times you may choose not to obey God's laws. This hurts your friendship with God and others.

You can ask the Holy Spirit to help you see where you have made wrong choices. You can think about your thoughts, words, and actions. This prayerful way of looking at your life is called an examination of conscience. These are a few questions that will help you.

Words of Faith

Contrition is being sorry for sin and wanting to live better.

Examination of Conscience

1. Did you put God first in your life?
2. Did you use God's name in a holy way?
3. Did you keep Sunday a holy day?
4. Did you obey your parents and teachers?
5. Did you hurt another person on purpose?

After you think about your sins, you can tell God that you are sorry. Then tell him you will try harder to live by his commandments. This means you have **contrition** for your sins.

Activity: Share Your Faith

Think: What is another question you can ask yourself during an examination of conscience?

Share: Talk about some questions with a partner.

Act: Write two questions on a separate piece of paper.

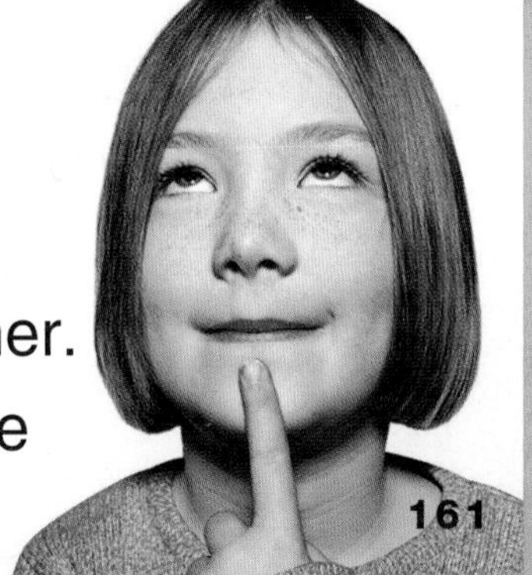

The Sacrament of Reconciliation

Focus How does the Church celebrate God's forgiveness?

After examining your conscience and being sorry for your sins, you are ready to celebrate the Church's Sacrament of Forgiveness. This sacrament is also called the **Sacrament of Reconciliation**, or the Sacrament of Penance. Each time you receive the sacrament, you receive God's forgiveness and celebrate your friendship with God.

You can receive the Sacrament of Reconciliation individually or as part of a parish celebration. These are the steps to celebrate the Sacrament of Reconciliation individually. The priest will help you if you forget a step.

When does your parish celebrate this sacrament?

Steps in the Sacrament

1. **Welcome Rites** The priest greets you with the Sign of the Cross.
2. **Scripture Reading** The priest reads, or you quietly read, a Bible passage about forgiveness.
3. **Confession and Penance** You tell your sins to the priest, who can never tell anyone your sins. He talks with you about ways you can do better. He gives you a **penance**.
4. **Contrition** You pray an Act of Contrition.
5. **Absolution** The priest forgives, or absolves, your sins in the name of the Father, the Son, and the Holy Spirit.
6. **Closing** The priest prays, "Give thanks to the Lord, for he is good." You say, "His mercy endures forever." You go out to do better and to make up for what you have done wrong.

Words of Faith

In the **Sacrament of Reconciliation** God's forgiveness for sin is given through the Church.

A **penance** is a prayer or an act to make up for sin.

Absolution is the forgiveness of sin you receive from God through the Church in the Sacrament of Reconciliation.

Activity — Connect Your Faith

Show Good Actions
Show a child doing good actions after receiving the Sacrament of Reconciliation.

Explore

An Act of Contrition

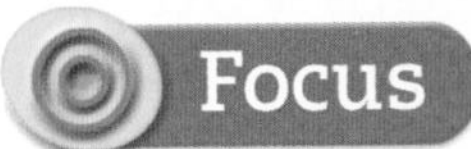

How do you tell God you are sorry for sin?

In the Sacrament of Penance and Reconciliation, you pray an Act of Contrition. The words of this prayer tell God that you are sorry for what you have done and that you want him to help you do better in the future.

Words of the Prayer	What They Mean
My God, I am sorry for my sins with all my heart.	God, I know I have done wrong, and I am very sorry.
In choosing to do wrong and failing to do good,	Sometimes I have done wrong things on purpose. Sometimes I haven't done good things that I should have done.
I have sinned against you, whom I should love above all things.	You have asked me to love you with my whole heart, soul, mind, and strength, and I haven't done that.
I firmly intend, with your help, to do penance,	I promise to do the actions and say the prayers that the priest gives me. I need your help.
to sin no more, and to avoid whatever leads me to sin.	From now on, I will try hard to make better choices. I will stay away from people and things that lead me away from you.
Our Savior Jesus Christ suffered and died for us.	Jesus died on the cross to save us from the power of sin.
In his name, my God, have mercy.	I believe what Jesus taught us about you, his loving Father. Please forgive me.

? What are some other ways you can tell God you are sorry for your sins?

Activity

Live Your Faith

Think About Choices Read each action. If you think the action is a good choice, draw a happy face next to it. If you think it is a bad choice, draw a sad face next to it.

Ask a lonely child to play.

Make fun of someone.

Copy a classmate's homework.

Listen to your teacher.

Ignore someone.

Say thank you.

Pray.

Help clean up after dinner.

Skip your chores.

Talk with a Partner Pick one of the choices you drew a sad face for. Write what you could do to make a better choice.

Prayer for Forgiveness

Gather and begin with the Sign of the Cross.

Leader: God our Father, be with us now as we think about ways we can be better.

Sing together.

It's me, it's me, Oh Lord,
Standin' in the need of prayer.
It's me, it's me, Oh Lord,
Standin' in the need of prayer.

"Standin' in the Need of Prayer" African-American Spiritual

Group 1: We have not been as helpful as we could be.

All: **But you love and come to us.**

Group 2: We have not been as kind to others as we could be.

All: **But you love and come to us.**

Leader: Let us give thanks for God's forgiveness and pray the Act of Contrition.

Based on Rite of Penance

Review

WORD BANK

Reconciliation
penance
Absolution

A Work with Words Use a word from the Word Bank to complete each sentence.

1. ______________ is the forgiveness of sin you receive from God through the Church in the Sacrament of Reconciliation.

2. In the Sacrament of ______________ God's forgiveness for sin is given through the Church.

3. A ______________ is a prayer or an act to make up for sin.

B Check Understanding Use the numbers 1 through 6. Put the steps of the celebration of the Sacrament of Reconciliation in order.

4. Step ______ I listen to a story of forgiveness.
5. Step ______ The priest greets me with the Sign of the Cross.
6. Step ______ I tell my sins to the priest.
7. Step ______ The priest forgives my sins.
8. Step ______ I pray an Act of Contrition.
9. Step ______ I try to do better.

C Make Connections Complete the sentence.

10. The Sacrament of Reconciliation celebrates ____
____.

Family Faith

Catholics Believe

- In the Sacrament of Reconciliation you receive God's forgiveness.
- The sacrament also celebrates your friendship with God and the Church.

SCRIPTURE

Jesus' parable of the unforgiving servant (Matthew 18:21–35) is about forgiving others.

GO online **www.osvcurriculum.com**
For weekly scripture readings and seasonal resources

Activity

Live Your Faith

Examine Your Conscience As part of the family evening ritual, take some time to think about events of the day.

- Work together to develop questions to help each person examine his or her conscience.
- Allow time for each person to silently ask God for forgiveness.
- Pray together an Act of Contrition.

▲ Saint Paul, first century

People of Faith

Paul did not like Christians. He helped put them in jail. One day, Paul heard Jesus say, "Why do you persecute me?" Paul realized that he had done wrong. That very minute, Paul stopped hurting Christians. Instead, he went everywhere telling people about Jesus, his Lord and Savior. Many people became followers of Jesus because of Paul's work. Paul was put in jail for believing in Jesus. The feast day of Saint Paul is July 25.

Family Prayer

Saint Paul, pray for us that we may follow Jesus and change for the better. Lead us to Jesus, our Lord and Savior. Amen.

In Unit 4 your child is learning about the CHURCH.

 CCC *See Catechism of the Catholic Church 1422-1424 for further reading on chapter content.*

Chapter 12

The Church Year

Invite

Let Us Pray

Leader: Lord, we praise you every day.
"Only goodness and love will pursue me
all the days of my life."
Psalm 23:6

All: Lord, we praise you every day. Amen.

Activity Let's Begin

Puzzling Questions

Dear Mr. Sun,

Why is it dark in the morning when I go to school in winter? Why is it light in the morning when I want to sleep late in the summer?

Why is it so hot in summer that I need to swim?

Why is it so cool in fall that I must wear a jacket?

Why do you melt the snow in winter? Why don't you melt the flowers in spring?

Your friend,
Josie Luna

• Which season do you like best?

____

____

Draw a Season Draw a picture of yourself doing something you enjoy in your favorite season.

The Church's Seasons

Focus What is celebrated in the Church year?

During the year the Church's **liturgy** celebrates the events in the life of Jesus. The Church celebrates the light of Jesus throughout the Church year.

SCRIPTURE

Jesus spoke to his followers saying, "I am the light of the world. Whoever follows me will not walk in darkness, but will have the light of life."

John 8:12

During the four weeks of Advent, the Church gets ready to celebrate Jesus' birth. You tell God that you want to get better at loving him and others. Just as the seasons have different colors, so do the Church's seasons. The color for Advent is violet. It is a sign of getting ready and change of heart.

The pink candle is for joy that Christmas is almost here.

Why is only one candle pink in the Advent wreath?

Christmas

The three weeks of the Christmas Season celebrate Jesus' presence in the world. The Son of God came so all people could know his Father's love. The Christmas celebrations help people love Jesus and other people more. White is the color for the Christmas Season. It is a sign of great joy.

Ordinary Time

Ordinary Time comes twice during the Church year. The first time is after the Christmas Season. The second is after the Easter Season. During these times you learn more about Jesus and grow as his follower. Green is the season's color because it is the color of growth.

Words of Faith

The **liturgy** is the public worship of the Church. It includes the sacraments and forms of daily prayer.

Activity — Share Your Faith

Think: What seasons of the Church year do you know?

Share: Talk about the seasons. How are they alike? How are they different? What season is the Church in now?

Act: Write about a Church season you really like to celebrate.

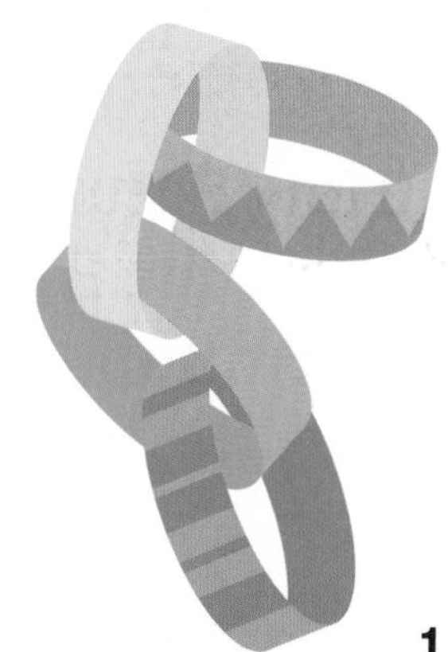

Explore

The Greatest Celebration

Focus What is the greatest feast of the Church year?

The Season of Lent is a preparation for the important feast of Easter. For forty days and six Sundays, the Church's color is violet. As during Advent, you are asked to make changes that will help you grow closer to Jesus. You are to pray more often and help others.

The Three Days

The three days before Easter are the holiest days of the Church year. On Holy Thursday the Church celebrates Jesus' gift of the Eucharist at the Last Supper. It is a joyous occasion, so the color is white.

On Good Friday the Church gives thanks to Jesus as Savior. The color is red because Jesus died for all people.

Holy Saturday evening begins the Easter celebration. For this joyous feast, the color is white.

Easter

Every Sunday the Church celebrates the **Resurrection**, when Jesus was raised from the dead. But each year, the Church celebrates the Resurrection of Jesus for fifty days from Easter to Pentecost. Easter is the greatest feast of the Church year. The color during this season is white.

The last ten days of this season celebrate Jesus' promise to send the Holy Spirit. Pentecost is the celebration of the Holy Spirit coming to the Apostles. For this feast the color red is used as a sign of the power of the Holy Spirit.

Why do you think Easter is the greatest feast of the Church year?

Words of Faith

The **Resurrection** is the mystery of Jesus being raised from death.

Activity Connect Your Faith

Find the Hidden Word Color the X's yellow and O's blue and red to discover the Easter word.

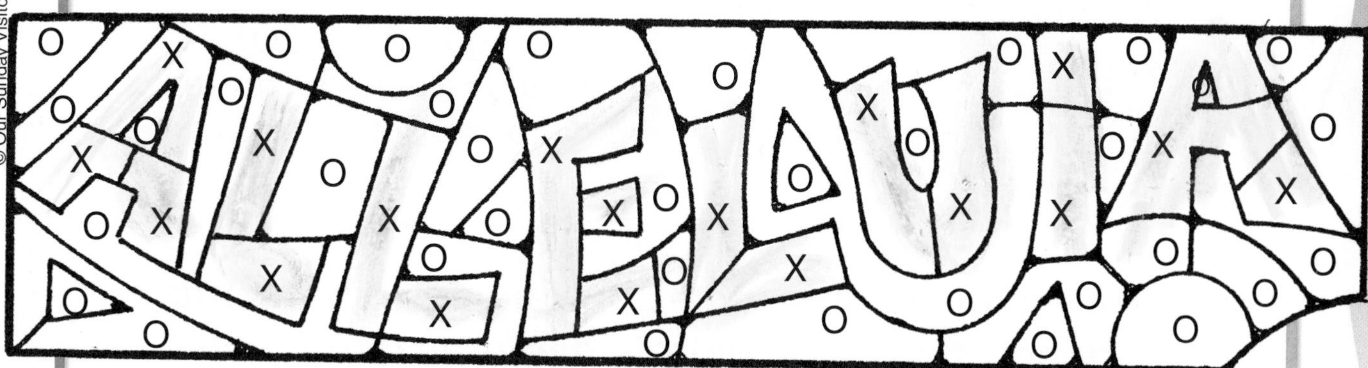

Explore

Showing Our Colors

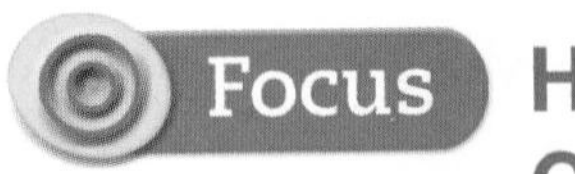

How do you know what Church season it is?

Families often decorate their homes for holidays. In the fall you see orange pumpkins and golden ears of corn. Spring banners wave in the breeze and show off the colors of red robins, orange tulips, and yellow daffodils.

Your parish family uses colors to celebrate the Church's seasons and feasts, too. Here are some places you may see colors of the season used in your parish church.

Vestments		The special robes worn by the priest and the deacon for Mass
Altar Hangings		The cloth that covers the altar is always white, but sometimes another drape in the color of the season hangs in front of the altar.
Banners		Like flags, these colorful hangings can be carried in procession.
Flowers and Plants		Flowers and plants that decorate the church can tell you what season it is.

? Why do you think the Church uses colors and decorations to celebrate seasons and feasts?

Activity

Live Your Faith

Decorate the Church What Church season is it now? Color the drawing to show which season the Church is celebrating now.

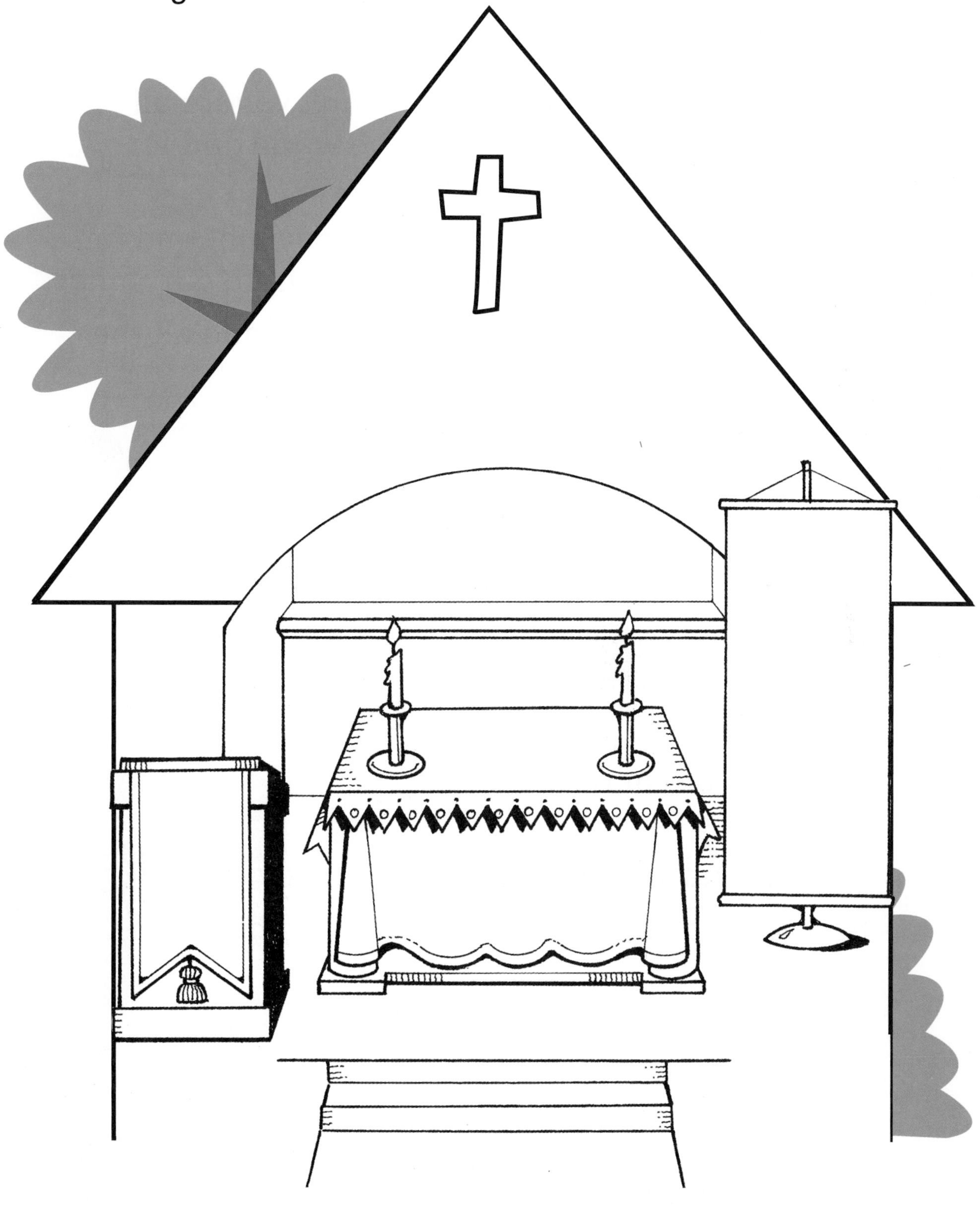

Prayer of Praise

Gather and begin with the Sign of the Cross.

Leader: God our Father, we thank you for all that is beautiful in the world and for the happiness you give us.

Reader 1: We praise you for your daylight and for your word which gives light to our minds.

Reader 2: We praise you for the earth and all the people on it.

All: **We know that you are good. You love us and do great things for us.**

From EP for Children, #1

Sing together the refrain.

Dance, then, wherever you
  may be,
I am the Lord of the Dance,
  said he,
And I'll lead you all, wherever you may be,
And I'll lead you all in the Dance, said he.

"I Danced in the Morning" © 1963 Stainer & Bell Ltd.

Review

A **Work with Words** Match the description of the season in Column I with the letter of the correct season in Column 2.

Column I	Column 2
1. Three weeks of joy that celebrate Jesus' presence in the world ______	a. Advent
2. The season that comes twice during the year ______	b. Christmas
3. Four weeks of getting ready to celebrate Jesus' birth ______	c. Lent
4. The season that celebrates Jesus' Resurrection ______	d. Ordinary Time
5. Forty days of praying and helping others as a way to prepare for Easter ______	e. Easter

B **Check Understanding** Write **T** if the sentence is TRUE. Write **F** if the sentence is FALSE.

6. Banners are special robes worn by the priest. ______
7. The cloth that covers the altar is white. ______
8. Flowers and plants that decorate the church can tell you what season it is. ______
9. The Church's seasons have different colors. ______
10. What is the Church year?

____

____

Family Faith

Catholics Believe

- The Church year celebrates the life, death, and Resurrection of Jesus.
- The Resurrection is the mystery of Jesus being raised from death.

SCRIPTURE

Read Ecclesiastes 3:1–8 to find out what God says about time.

GO online **www.osvcurriculum.com**
For weekly scripture readings and seasonal resources

Activity

Live Your Faith

Make a Poster Look around your church. Talk about the colors and signs of the Church season that is being celebrated now. Work together to make a poster of the Church season to display in your home.

▲ Pope Saint Victor, 197–199 A.D.

People of Faith

Pope Saint Victor was one of three popes from Africa. He decided with the bishops that Easter must be celebrated on Sunday. Saint Victor also declared that the Mass should be celebrated in the language of the people. At that time the language was Latin. The Church celebrates his feast day on July 28.

Family Prayer

Pope Saint Victor, ask God to help us bring his message to our friends and family. Amen.

In Unit 4 your child is learning about the CHURCH.

 CCC *See Catechism of the Catholic Church 1188–1195 for further reading on chapter content.*

DISCOVER

Catholic Social Teaching:

The Dignity of Work and the Rights of Workers

In this unit you learned that God is with us all the time. We celebrate God's life and love in the sacraments. We celebrate with Jesus throughout the Church year.

Respect for Workers

Work is an important part of human life. People work to earn money for the things they need. Workers take pride in doing their jobs well.

Jesus learned about work from his foster father, Joseph. Joseph was a carpenter who made beautiful and useful things from wood. Jesus also watched his mother, Mary, as she worked hard to make a loving home for the family.

The Church teaches that all kinds of work are important. Workers and bosses have to treat one another with respect. Everyone who works deserves to be paid fairly. No one should work in unsafe conditions.

Who are some of the workers who help make your life safe, comfortable, and interesting?

CONNECT

With the Call to Justice

We Wear Their Work

All workers should be treated with respect. Let's look at what some U.S. college students did to help.

Do you have a favorite tee-shirt? Most young people do! But have you ever thought about where that shirt was made?

Many clothes are made here in the United States. Other clothes sold here are made in other countries around the world. Often these factory workers work long hours for little pay. They are not treated with respect.

Many groups in this country are trying to do something about these bad working conditions. One group trying to help is the Worker Rights Consortium (con-SORE-tee-um). They ask American colleges and universities to buy items only from companies who treat their workers well.

The next time you wear your favorite tee-shirt, think about the person who made that shirt. Ask God to make his or her working conditions better.

? How does the Worker Rights Consortium help workers in clothing factories?

Lemonade
5¢
Help Workers

Reach Out!

SERVE
Your Community

Do Your Part

You may think you are too young to help change the lives of workers. Because of you, workers may get better working conditions and the respect of the people for whom they work. Here are some ideas you and your family might try.

Skip-a-Snack Save the money you might use to buy snacks at school or at a movie for one month. Ask your family to help you send the money to the Worker Rights Consortium or Catholic Charities to be used to help workers.

CALENDAR
POP CORN

Yard Sale Organize a yard sale with your family. Invite friends' families to join, too. Sell lemonade and cookies. Make cards or other crafts to sell. Tell your customers you are raising money for the rights of workers around the world.

Make a Difference

Write a Class Letter Workers in this country often need help, too. With your teacher's help, write a class letter to the president or to your state senators. Ask elected leaders to help pass stronger laws that protect the health and safety of workers of all ages.

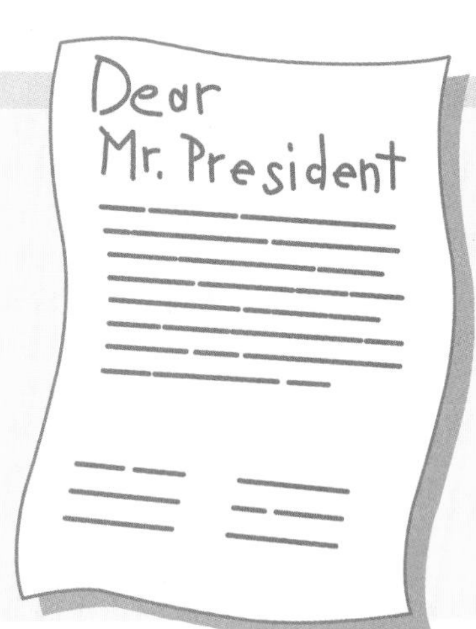

Unit 4 Review

A **Work with Words** Complete each sentence with the correct word from the Word Bank.

WORD BANK

Sacraments
Grace
Liturgy
Absolution
Contrition

1. ______________ is the public worship of the Church.

2. ______________ are holy signs that come from Jesus and give us life.

3. ______________ is being sorry for sin and wanting to live better.

4. ______________ is sharing in God's life.

5. ______________ is the forgiveness of sin from God in the Sacrament of Reconciliation.

B **Check Understanding** Circle the correct answer.

6. What does the word Resurrection mean?

   Jesus died **Jesus was born** **Jesus rose from death**

7. What does Pentecost celebrate?

   death of Jesus **life of Jesus** **coming of Holy Spirit**

8. What is the first sacrament you receive?

   Confirmation **Baptism** **Eucharist**

9. What sacrament celebrates God's forgiveness?

   Anointing **Reconciliation** **Eucharist**

10. What does Christmas celebrate?

    death of Jesus **life of Jesus** **birth of Jesus**

Circle **T** if the sentence is TRUE. Circle **F** if the sentence is FALSE.

11. In the sacraments you receive grace. **T** **F**

12. Grace is God's own life and love. **T** **F**

13. Confirmation is the first sacrament you receive. **T** **F**

14. You can receive the Sacrament of Reconciliation only with the parish community. **T** **F**

15. In the Sacrament of Reconciliation you receive God's forgiveness. **T** **F**

C **Make Connections** Describe each of the things used in church during the Church year.

16. Colors

____

17. Vestments

____

18. Altar hangings

____

19. Banners

____

20. Flowers and plants

____

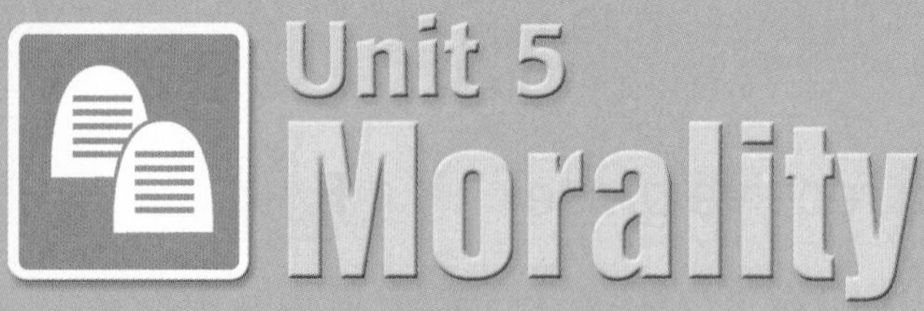

Unit 5 Morality

In this unit you will...

learn that Jesus told us that the kingdom of God is where we discover love, peace and justice. All are welcome in the kingdom. We are Jesus' followers. He taught us how to pray. We share in his life and work. We share the good news with the world. We pray, we forgive, and we love.

Faith in Action!

Catholic Social Teaching Principle:
Solidarity of the Human Family

Chapter 13 Care for All People

Let Us Pray

Leader: Lord, we praise you for your love.
"Your love for me is great."
Psalm 86:13

All: Lord, we praise you for your love. Amen.

Come In "Will she know me? What will she say?" I wondered as I knocked on the principal's door.

"What a surprise! Hello, Omar, welcome to my office."

I handed the principal the note to leave early.

"Have a good time with your grandmother this afternoon, Omar. We'll miss you."

- How did the principal make Omar feel welcome?

Make a List With a partner, make a list of some people who might visit your school or parish. Think of one way you could make each visitor feel welcome.

Jesus' Example

How did Zacchaeus show his faith in God?

The principal made Omar feel welcome. Here is a time that Jesus showed that God welcomes everyone.

SCRIPTURE

Luke 19:1–8

A Surprise Guest

Word went out uphill and down,
Jesus was coming to Jericho town.

Zacchaeus, you know, was too short
to see,
So he scurried right up a sycamore tree.

"Zacchaeus, come down, come down,
I say.
Let's have dinner at your house today."

Jesus and Zacchaeus walked by the
crowd
who grumbled and mumbled and said
out loud:

"He is a sinner and he is a snitch.
He took our money. That's why he is rich."

Zacchaeus proclaimed in a loud,
clear tone,
"To the poor I will give half of all that
I own."

Then Jesus said, "God's love has no end.
My friend, Zacchaeus, is also God's friend.

Put away your frowns. Be full of cheer.
God's love and kindness are truly here.

God calls everyone, the
small and the great.

So, come gather around.
Come celebrate!"

Based on Luke 19:1–8

Words of Faith

Faith is belief in God and all that he has told about himself.

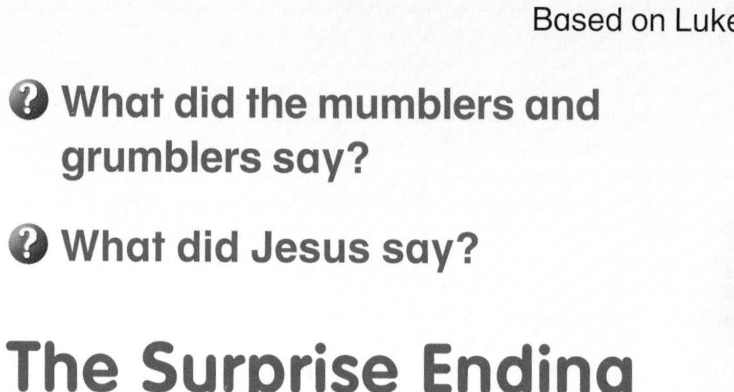

What did the mumblers and grumblers say?

What did Jesus say?

The Surprise Ending

Jesus saw that Zacchaeus had **faith** in God. Zacchaeus wanted to follow Jesus. So Jesus surprised all. He welcomed Zacchaeus to share in God's love.

Activity Share Your Faith

Think: Imagine that Jesus has come to your house. What would you say and do?

Share: Tell a partner how you would feel.

Act: Take turns role playing this with your partner.

All Are Welcome

 **Who does Jesus invite to God's kingdom?**

It did not matter to Jesus how old a person was or how tall. Jesus welcomed everyone to talk with him.

 Matthew 19:13–15

Little Children

People often brought their children to Jesus. The disciples said, "Don't bother Jesus. He is too busy!" But Jesus said, "Let the children come to me . . . for the kingdom of heaven belongs to such as these."

Jesus welcomed the children and blessed them. Then he sent the children on their way.

Based on Matthew 19:13–15

? How did Jesus treat the children?

In God's Kingdom

Another name for the kingdom of heaven is the **kingdom of God**. Jesus invites everyone to enter the kingdom of love and peace. Jesus knew how to make people feel welcome. Many people came to him for help and healing. Some people were like Zacchaeus. They thought Jesus wouldn't care about them. Jesus taught that all people are welcome in God's kingdom.

Like Jesus, the Catholic Church welcomes all people. Every Sunday there are people who welcome each Church member before Mass begins. These welcomers can be men, women, or children.

How are you welcomed by others?

Words of Faith

The **kingdom of God** is love, peace, and justice for all.

Activity Connect Your Faith

Trace Your Foot Cut out the traced foot. Write your name on it. Using everyone's footprints, make a trail in the classroom leading to your prayer center.

With God

Focus Who is welcome in God's kingdom?

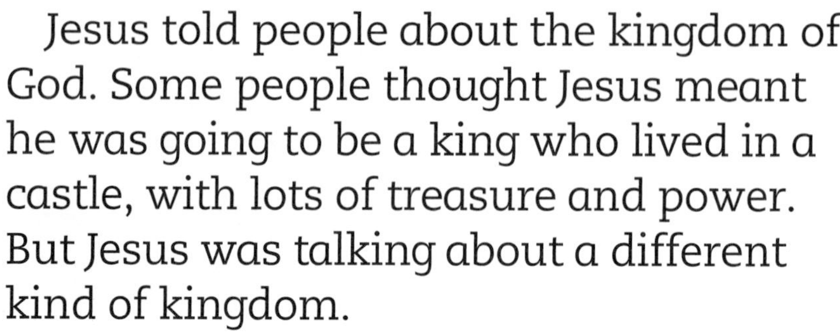

Jesus told people about the kingdom of God. Some people thought Jesus meant he was going to be a king who lived in a castle, with lots of treasure and power. But Jesus was talking about a different kind of kingdom.

God's kingdom is a world of peace, love, and joy. By his kindness and care, Jesus showed that everyone is welcome in God's kingdom.

God's kingdom will be complete at the end of time, but you have already been given an invitation. When you were baptized, you were welcomed into God's kingdom. When you go to Mass, you are celebrating the banquet of God's kingdom.

- Does it matter whether you are short or tall? NO!
- Does it matter whether you are poor or rich? NO!
- Does it matter what color your eyes are, or your hair, or your skin? NO!
- Does it matter whether you are good at soccer or you love to read? NO!

? **What other things don't matter in God's kingdom?**

Activity

Live Your Faith

Write an Invitation Fill in the blanks to complete the invitation. Then decorate the invitation with colorful designs.

You Are Invited!

Jesus invites

____

to the Kingdom of

______________________.

Come this Sunday to join

____

at the banquet of God's Kingdom,

the ______________________,

at the parish church of

______________________________.

Prayer of Welcome

Gather and make the Sign of the Cross.

Leader: God our Father, we gather together in Jesus' name.

Reader 1: When we welcome a friend,

All: Jesus' love shows through us.

Reader 2: When we welcome a child who is left out,

All: Jesus' love shows through us.

Reader 3: When we take extra time to help,

All: Jesus' love shows through us.

Leader: Let us pray.

Bow your heads as the leader prays.

All: Amen.

Sing together.

Fill us with your love,
O Lord,
and we will sing
for joy!

"Psalm 90: Fill Us with Your Love"
© 1969, 1981, and 1997, ICEL

Review

A Work with Words Fill in the blank with the correct word from the Word Bank.

WORD BANK

welcomes
kingdom of God
Faith
children
Zacchaeus

1. ________________ became Jesus' friend.
2. Jesus ________________ everyone.
3. Jesus blessed the ________________.
4. Everyone is invited into the ________________.
5. ________________ is belief in God.

B Check Understanding Circle the correct answer.

6. _______ told people about the kingdom of God.
   Zacchaeus **Jesus** **The children**
7. Jesus showed that everyone is welcome in _______.
   other countries **every club** **God's kingdom**
8. _______ welcomes you into God's kingdom.
   The priest **Baptism** **Mary**
9. Mass celebrates the _______ of God's kingdom.
   banquet **beginning** **end**

C Make Connections Write your answer on the line.

10. What is the kingdom of God like?

____

Family Faith

Catholics Believe

- The kingdom of God is love, peace, and justice for all.
- Everyone is welcome in God's kingdom and the Catholic Church.

SCRIPTURE

Matthew 18:1–5 tells of the special place of children in God's kingdom.

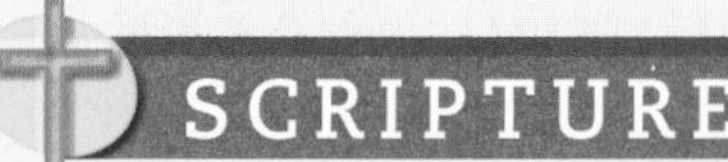

GO online **www.osvcurriculum.com**
For weekly scripture readings and seasonal resources

Activity

Live Your Faith

Do Acts of Kindness Write the name of each family member on a separate slip of paper. Put all the slips in a cup.

- Have each family member draw a name.
- For one week, each member of the family is to do small acts of kindness for the person whose name he or she drew.

People of Faith

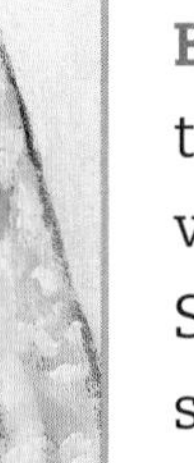

▲ **Saint Brigid of Kildare, d. c. 525**

Brigid was a nun who dedicated her life to God. Others soon joined her. Brigid went all around Ireland. She walked. She traveled by horse and cart. She sailed in a boat on the Irish Sea. Everywhere Brigid went, she spoke of the love of God. She was known for her kindness and mercy to everyone. Saint Brigid is a patron saint of Ireland. Her feast day is February 1.

Family Prayer

Saint Brigid, pray for us that we may be strong and lively in the love of God. Amen.

In Unit 5 your child is learning about MORALITY.

CCC See Catechism of the Catholic Church 543, 544 for further reading on chapter content.

Chapter 14 Share the Good News

Leader: Jesus, you are with us always.
"Christ lives in me."
Galatians 2:20

All: Jesus, you are with us always. Amen.

Someone Special Justin keeps stories and pictures of his uncle.

Uncle Matt is a hockey player. He can skate faster than anyone Justin knows. His uncle sets goals and works hard to reach them.

Now Uncle Matt's team is going to play in the regional finals. Justin wants everybody to know about his Uncle Matt.

- How do you think Justin shares the news about his Uncle Matt?

Write About Good News Write about a time when you had some good news to share.

Explore

Live as Followers

What did Jesus ask his followers to do?

Justin wanted everyone to know about his Uncle Matt. Jesus wanted everyone to know about God his Father.

Jesus knew that the work of spreading his message would be hard. His followers would need his help. He made a promise. If they stayed close to him, they would do many good things.

SCRIPTURE John 15:4–5

The Vine and the Branches

Jesus told his disciples "Remain in me, as I remain in you. A branch cannot bear fruit unless it remains on the vine. You cannot bear fruit and do good things unless you remain in me."

Jesus said, "I am the vine, you are the branches. Whoever remains in me and I in him will bear much fruit."

From John 15:4–5

How can you stay close to Jesus?

The Message to Others

After Jesus was raised from the dead, he gathered with his disciples. He wanted them to share in his work.

SCRIPTURE

"Go, therefore, and make disciples of all nations, baptizing them in the name of the Father, and of the Son, and of the Holy Spirit, teaching them to observe all that I have commanded you. And behold I am with you always."

Matthew 28:19–20

The Holy Spirit guided Jesus' followers to places that they had never seen. The Spirit strengthened them to **proclaim** the good news. They told the people everything that Jesus had taught them.

Words of Faith

To **proclaim** Jesus is to tell about him with loving words and actions.

Activity Share Your Faith

Think: What do you think Jesus' followers told others about him?

Share: With a partner talk about these things.

Act: Write one thing you can do to show you are a follower of Jesus.

___

___

Explore

Jesus' Followers Today

Focus **How do people share Jesus' message?**

Faith Fact

There are over 1 billion Catholics in the world.

Jesus' followers still bring his message to the world. People do this in different ways. Here are some people who serve Jesus and share his love with others.

- Sister Rosa helps children learn more about God.
- Mr. Rodriguez teaches songs so that children can sing to God.
- Parents and grandparents teach their children to pray.

- Father Ed celebrates Mass and gives the people the gift of Jesus.
- Deacon Jerry helps in the parish by baptizing people.

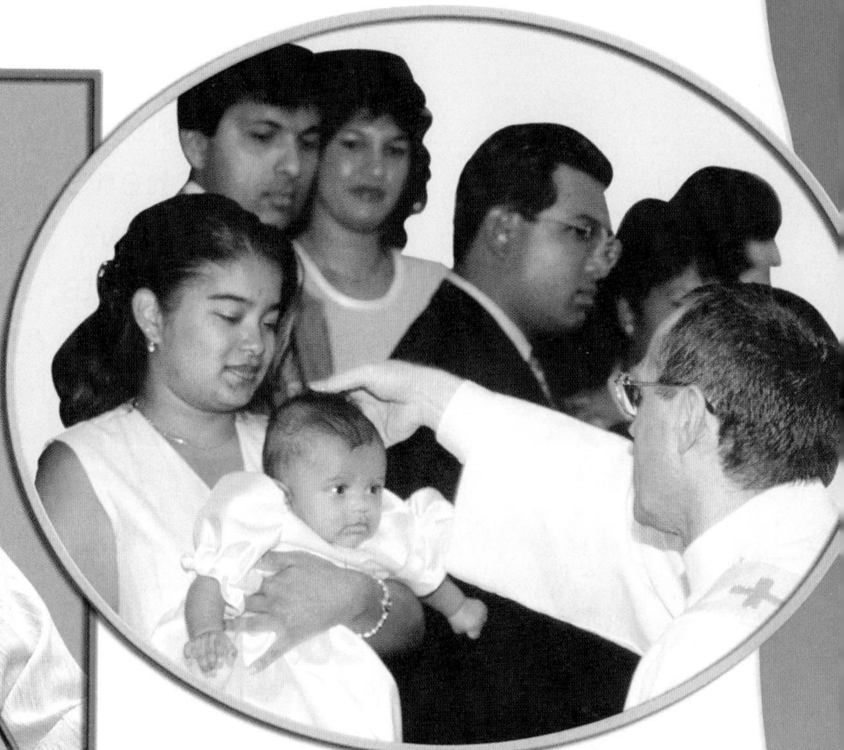

Activity Connect Your Faith

Draw one way someone in your parish helps.

Use Your Gifts

Focus How can you share the good news of Jesus?

Jesus asked all of his followers to share the good news. He told them to use the gifts God gave them to do this. God has given you gifts, too. You have the gifts of time, talent, and treasure to help you share good news.

Your Gifts		
The gift	**What it is**	**How you can use it to share the good news of Jesus**
Time	All the minutes of your day, which you can choose to use generously or selfishly	Do extra chores at home. Run errands for a neighbor. Spend time with an older or younger family member.
Talent	All the things you like to do and things you do well, which you can use generously or selfishly	Teach someone to play your favorite game or sport. Read or tell a story to a younger child. Make a card or drawing for someone who is sick.
Treasure	All the things you have, which you can use generously or selfishly	Let a friend borrow a toy. Collect extra clothes and toys for people who have less. Help collect money to give to people who are poor or hungry.

How is sharing your gifts a good way to share the good news of Jesus?

Activity

Live Your Faith

The Good News in Stories

Jesus told stories as a way of sharing the good news. Think about two stories of Jesus you heard this year. With a partner, answer the questions about each story.

The Good Samaritan

How did the Samaritan use his gifts?

How could you use your gifts to bring good news to someone in need?

The Forgiving Father

How did the father use his gifts?

How could you use your gifts to bring good news to someone who needs forgiveness?

Tell Your Own Story Write or tell your own story about someone who uses his or her gifts of time, talent, or treasure to bring good news.

Prayer of Thanksgiving

Gather and begin with the Sign of the Cross.

Leader: We praise and thank you, O Lord
for the many people who share your
good news.

Blessed be the name of the Lord.

All: Now and forever.

Leader: We praise and thank you, O
Lord for the people who help
in our parish.

Blessed be the name of the Lord.

All: Now and forever. Amen.

Sing together.

We are sent two by two.
Sent as church in the world.
Sent to share God's
good news,
Sing and tell, spread
the Word.

"Two By Two" © 2000, GIA Publications, Inc.

Review

A **Work with Words** Circle the correct answer.

1. Jesus said to make _______ of all nations.

   friends **slaves** **disciples**

2. The _______ was sent to help Jesus' disciples.

   kingdom **Holy Spirit** **priest**

3. Jesus told his followers to _______ all nations.

   baptize **confirm** **shake hands with**

4. Jesus is the _______ and we are the branches.

   vine **leaves** **soil**

B **Check Understanding** Draw a line from Column A to the best ending in Column B.

Column A	Column B
5. Jesus told his followers to use	a. God.
6. Jesus asked all his followers to share	b. the gifts God gave them.
7. You can use the gifts of	c. the good news.
8. All of our gifts come from	d. time, talent, and treasure.

C **Make Connections** Write your answer on the lines.

9-10. Jason is a good reader. His brother is having trouble reading. Name two gifts Jason can use to help him.

Family Faith

Catholics Believe

- Jesus' disciples share in his life and in his work.
- Jesus is with us always.

SCRIPTURE

Read 1 Corinthians 12:4–6 to learn what Saint Paul says about different ways to serve God.

GO online **www.osvcurriculum.com**
For weekly scripture readings and seasonal resources

Activity

Live Your Faith

Loving Actions As a family, choose a loving action that will be practiced by every family member for a week. Emphasize that a smile or an act of courtesy may brighten someone's day. At the end of the week, talk about how the family members feel about the loving actions.

▲ **Blessed Mother Teresa of Calcutta, 1910–1997**

People of Faith

A little girl named Agnes grew up to be **Mother Teresa**. She worked in India, far from her home. She cared for the poor and dying. She began a new group of sisters called the Missionaries of Charity. When people asked, "What can we do to help the people who are poor?" Mother Teresa told them to do their best for God right where they were. She said, "Do something beautiful for God." Mother Teresa was beatified by Pope Saint John Paul II in 2003.

Family Prayer

Dear Jesus, help us bear the fruit of your love. Help us do something beautiful for God, as Blessed Mother Teresa did. Amen.

In Unit 5 your child is learning about MORALITY.

 CCC *See Catechism of the Catholic Church 900, 904, and 905 for further reading on chapter content.*

Chapter 15

Pray as Jesus Did

Let Us Pray

Leader: Lord, hear us when we pray.

"Gladden the soul of your servant;
to you, LORD, I lift up my soul."

Psalm 86:4

All: Lord, hear us when we pray. Amen.

Activity Let's Begin

In Your Heart At Grandpa's house there was a statue of a man dressed in a long brown robe, holding a child.

"Who's that, Grandpa?" Joey asked.

Grandpa said, "That's Saint Anthony. There's a story that somebody once saw him praying. He was holding Jesus in his heart with so much love that it seemed as if the Christ Child was in his arms. Saint Anthony reminds me that God is in my heart, too."

- What things in your classroom remind you of God?

____

Draw a Reminder Draw things at home, at school, or in your parish church that remind you of God.

Time with God

How does Jesus want you to pray?

When you pray, you talk to and listen to God. The Bible says that Jesus prayed often. He wanted his followers to pray often, too.

SCRIPTURE Matthew 6:5–9

How to Pray

Jesus told his followers, "When you pray, go to your inner room, close the door, and pray to your Father in secret."

Jesus also told them, "Do not babble like the others, who think that they will be heard because of their many words . . . Your Father knows what you need before you ask him. This is how you are to pray:

Our Father in heaven,
hallowed be your name."

From Matthew 6:5–9

Where do you pray?

The Lord's Prayer

The name of the prayer that Jesus taught his followers is the **Lord's Prayer**. It is also called the "Our Father."

The **Lord's Prayer** is the prayer that Jesus taught his followers to pray to God the Father.

The Lord's Prayer	Meaning
Our Father who art in heaven, hallowed be thy name;	We praise God, our Father. We say God's name with love and respect.
thy kingdom come,	We pray that all people will know God's justice and peace.
thy will be done on earth as it is in heaven.	We will do what God wants, not what we want.
Give us this day our daily bread;	We ask God to give us what we need for now.
and forgive us our trespasses as we forgive those who trespass against us;	We ask God to be forgiving of us as we are of others.
and lead us not into temptation, but deliver us from evil.	We ask God to protect us from harm and keep us from sin.
Amen.	May it be so!

Activity Share Your Faith

Think: When do you pray the Lord's Prayer?

Share: Talk about times the Lord's Prayer is prayed.

Act: Draw a place where you can pray to God. Use a separate sheet of paper.

Explore

Ways to Pray

What do you say when you pray?

Prayer is a way to deepen your friendship with God. You can pray in many ways.

- You can worship, or adore, God.
- You can praise God for all the wonders of his creation.
- You can thank God for all his gifts.
- You can tell God you are sorry when you sin.
- You can ask God for whatever help you or others need.

You can say many things when you talk to God in prayer. Sometimes you can just be quiet and enjoy being in God's love.

Which type of prayer do you say often ?

What and When to Pray

You can use your words to pray. You can also use prayers that the Church and some of the saints have written. These prayers include the Hail Mary, the Glory to the Father, and prayers before meals.

You can pray when you are happy or sad or scared. You can pray when you are alone or with others. You can pray prayers that everyone knows, or you can make up prayers as you go.

Words of Faith

Sacramentals are blessings, objects, and actions that remind you of God and are made sacred through the prayers of the Church.

Prayer Reminders

You can pray when you see pictures or objects that remind you that God is with you. Objects such as a crucifix, a rosary, or holy water are **sacramentals**. Words of blessing and actions, such as the Sign of the Cross, are also sacramentals.

? What sacramentals do you have in your classroom? In your home?

Activity Connect Your Faith

Write a Prayer Write a short prayer of thanks to God. Tell what you are thankful for and why.

____

____

____

Explore

Your Own Words

How can you talk to God?

Prayer is talking and listening to God. Sometimes you talk to God using the words of prayers you have memorized, like the Lord's Prayer. Sometimes you pray in the words of the Bible, like the psalm verses that open each chapter in this book. But you can use your own words, too.

Here are some ideas of how you can talk to God.

A Prayer of Praise
God, the world you made is so amazing!

A Prayer of Worship
I love you, God, more than anyone or anything.

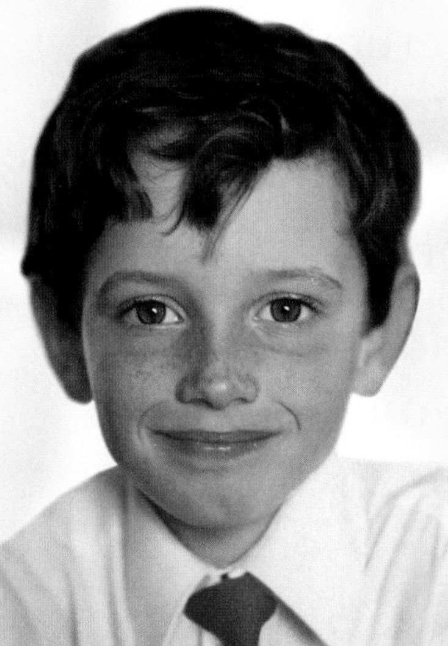

A Prayer of Thanksgiving
Thank you, God, for my family and friends, who share your love with me.

A Prayer of Sorrow for Sin
I really messed up this time, God. I'm so sorry. With your help, I know I can do better.

A Prayer Asking Help for Someone Else
God, please help Uncle Mike find a new job.

A Prayer Asking God to Help You
I'm scared, and I don't know what to do. God, please help me. I need to know you are with me.

What are some prayers you can pray?

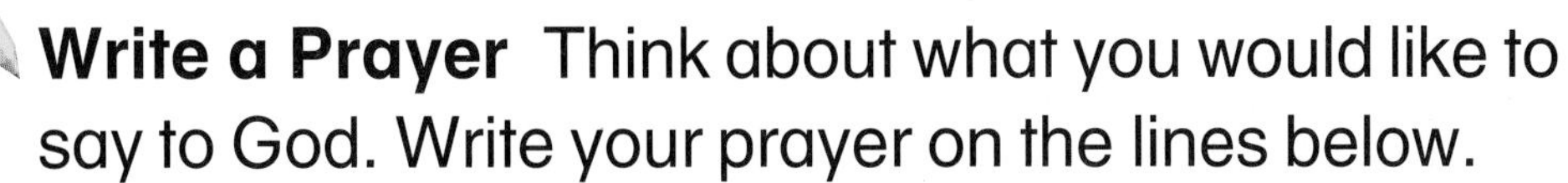

Write a Prayer Think about what you would like to say to God. Write your prayer on the lines below.

Dear God,

Love,

What kind of prayer did you write? Circle it. You may need to circle more than one kind of prayer.

A prayer of praise

A prayer of worship

A prayer of thanksgiving

A prayer of sorrow for sin

A prayer asking help for someone else

A prayer asking God to help you

The Lord's Prayer

Gather and begin with the Sign of the Cross.

Leader: Let us pray together the prayer that Jesus taught us.

All: Our Father, who art in heaven,
hallowed be thy name;
thy kingdom come;
thy will be done on earth
as it is in heaven.
Give us this day our daily bread;
and forgive us our trespasses
as we forgive those who
trespass against us;
and lead us not into
temptation,
but deliver us from evil.
Amen.

Sing together.

O Lord, hear my prayer,
O Lord, hear my prayer:
when I call answer me.
O Lord, hear my prayer,
O Lord, hear my prayer.

Review

A Work with Words Unscramble the words to find five good reasons to pray.

1. To worship, or DRAEO God. ____________________
2. To ESIARP God for his greatness. ____________________
3. To KNATH God for all his gifts. ____________________
4. To KAS God for what you need. ____________________
5. To LLTE God you are sorry. ____________________

B Check Understanding Draw a line from the prayers in Column A to the best description of that prayer in Column B.

Column A	Column B
6. God, you are the best! You give me everything I need.	a. prayer of thanksgiving
7. I hurt my friend's feelings, God. Please forgive me. I will make it up to her.	b. prayer of worship
8. I love you, God. You deserve all my love.	c. prayer asking help for someone else
9. Please, God, help Grandma get well.	d. prayer of praise
10. Thank you, God, for all my friends.	e. prayer of sorrow for sin

Family Faith

Catholics Believe

- Prayer is being with God in your mind and heart.
- Jesus taught his followers the Lord's Prayer.

SCRIPTURE

In Luke 11:9–13 you can read another one of Jesus' teachings about prayer.

www.osvcurriculum.com
For weekly scripture readings and seasonal resources

Activity

Live Your Faith

Start a Family Prayer Practice Different families have different ways of praying.

- Some pray to saints special to them.
- Others use sacramentals to pray together.
- Some have favorite customs to celebrate the seasons.
- As a group, come up with a special family prayer tradition.

▲ **David,** ca 1000 B.C.

People of Faith

David was a shepherd. He was the youngest of eight sons of Jesse. God chose him to be a great leader, a king of the Israelite people. David was also a musician. He wrote psalms of adoration, praise, thanksgiving, and need. Many of these are in the Bible. People recite many of David's psalms at Mass or during their daily prayers.

Family Prayer

Dear God, help us be like David each day. Remind us to praise and adore you through our prayers. Amen.

In Unit 5 your child is learning about MORALITY.

 CCC *See Catechism of the Catholic Church 2692–2696 for further reading on chapter content.*

DISCOVER

Catholic Social Teaching:

Solidarity of the Human Family

Faith in Action!

CATHOLIC SOCIAL TEACHING

In this unit you learned that everyone is welcome in God's kingdom of justice, love, and peace. You learned that Jesus sends you to share his good news at home, in school, and even to people you do not know.

One Human Family

The members of the human family, like the members of your family, may not all look alike. People have different skin colors. They speak different languages. They live in very different places. All humans are part of one family.

Just as you care for your brothers and sisters at home, Jesus sends us to care for our brothers and sisters around the world. That's one big job! One way to begin is to remember that everyone is made in God's image. Another way to care for our sisters and brothers around the world is to pray for them.

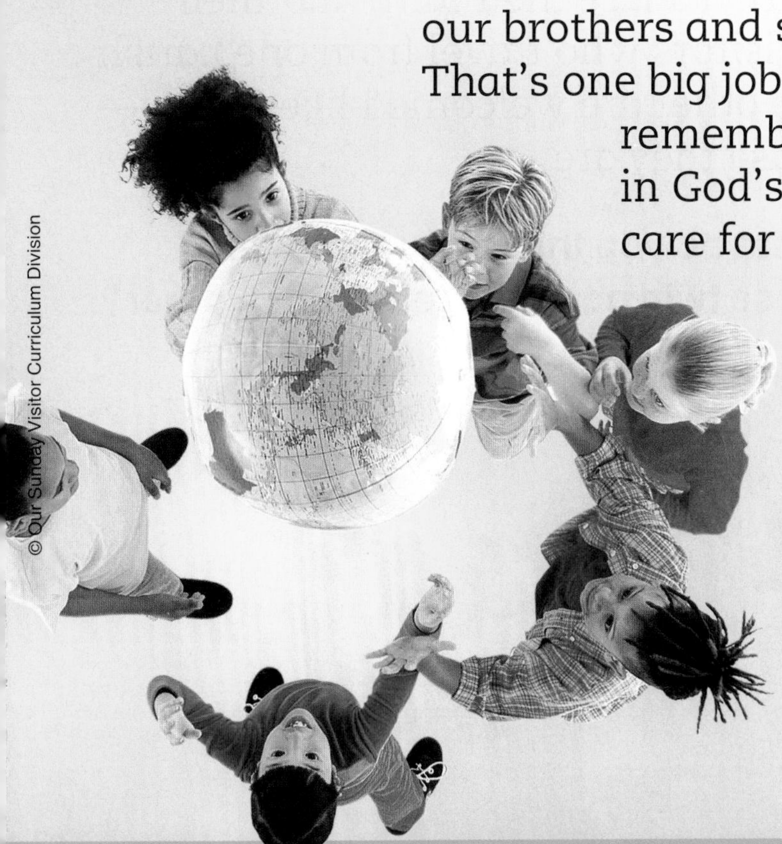

What are some other ways you can show that you care for all the members of the human family?

CONNECT

With the Call to Justice

Twins!

Caring for the human family starts right where we live. Let's look at how the people of one parish reached out to their sisters and brothers in another country.

Being a twin is a special blessing. Twins have a special way of being close. They grow up together and help one another.

Did you know that whole parishes can be twins? Holy Spirit Catholic Church in Virginia has a twin parish in the country of Haiti. The people of Holy Spirit Parish and the people of Our Lady of Mount Carmel Parish near Port-au-Prince, Haiti, chose to have a special, close relationship. The two parish communities help each other like twins.

Haiti is a poor country. The people of Holy Spirit Parish send gifts of food, medicine, and machinery to their twin parish. In return, the people of Our Lady of Mount Carmel Parish share their faith and their joy. Visitors who travel from one parish to the other are welcomed like family—because they are!

? What do you think the members of these twin parishes teach each other?

Reach Out!

SERVE

Your Community

Learn about the Human Family

One way to show that you care for all members of the human family is to learn about people in other parts of the world. Choose a country you want to learn about. Use library books or the Internet to find out about this country. Answer these questions on a separate sheet of paper.

1. What are three ways in which the people are like you?
2. What are three ways in which the people are different from you?
3. What could you learn from the people?
4. What could you teach them?

Make a Difference

Have a Cultural Festival Make a list of all the cultures and countries represented in your class. Hold a festival of cultures. Wear clothing from the country you learned about. Share special foods, music, and customs. Invite another class to celebrate with you.

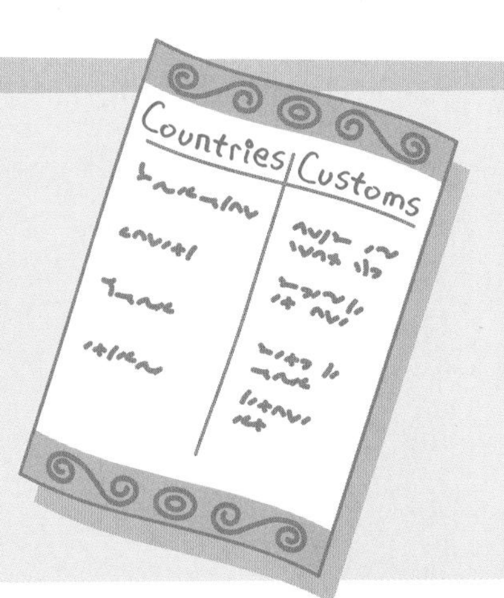

Unit 5 Review

A Work with Words Complete each sentence with the letter of the correct word or words from the Word Bank.

WORD BANK

a. proclaim
b. work
c. Faith
d. kingdom of God
e. Lord's

1. _______ is belief in God and all he has told us about himself.
2. The _______ is love, peace, and justice for all.
3. To _______ Jesus is to tell about him with loving words and actions.
4. The _______ Prayer is the prayer that Jesus taught us.
5. Jesus' disciples share in his life and _______.

B Check Understanding Circle the correct answer.

6. Who did Jesus call from the tree?

   Peter **John** **Zacchaeus**

7. Who does Jesus invite to the kingdom of God?

   everyone **saints** **Catholics**

8. Who is always guiding the Church's actions?

   saints **Holy Spirit** **disciples**

9. What name do we give to rosaries and holy water?

   sacraments **prayers** **sacramentals**

10. When will Jesus be with us?

    always **when we pray** **when we sin**

Circle **T** if the sentence is TRUE. Circle **F** if the sentence is FALSE.

11. Jesus was a king who lived in a castle with lots of treasure and power. **T F**

12. God's kingdom is a world of love, peace, and joy. **T F**

13. Jesus' followers no longer need to bring his message to the world. **T F**

14. Jesus asked all of his followers to share the good news. **T F**

15. Sometimes you can use memorized prayers to pray. **T F**

C Make Connections

16–20. Circle the words below that tell something about God's kingdom.

joy	**fighting**	**stealing**
shutting someone out	**lying**	**being unfair**
peace	**love**	**kindness**
wasting your gifts	**being selfish**	**welcome**

Unit 6 Sacraments

In this unit you will...

learn that the Mass is another name for the celebration of the Eucharist. The Mass has two parts: the Liturgy of the Word and the Liturgy of the Eucharist. At every Mass we hear God's word from the Bible and pray for the Church and the needs of the world. We remember Jesus' sacrifice and give thanks for it. He comes among us and renews his sacrifice. We receive his Body and Blood in Holy Communion.

Faith in Action!

Catholic Social Teaching Principle: Call to Family, Community, and Participation

Invite

Chapter 16

Gather to Worship

Let Us Pray

Leader: Jesus, thank you for being with us.
"For where two or three are gathered together in my name, there am I in the midst of them." Matthew 18:20

All: Jesus, thank you for being with us. Amen.

Activity Let's Begin

The Invitation Sam and his family were invited to a birthday party for their new neighbor, Paul. It was a big celebration. Paul's family and friends from all over the city and state were gathered. Sam was excited to meet some new people. Paul welcomed Sam and made him feel like part of the group. Together everyone had a great time.

- How do you think Paul made Sam feel like part of the group?

____

____

Write About Feeling Welcome Write about a time when someone made you feel welcome at a party or other event.

Gather to Celebrate

Focus Who gathers for the Mass?

Like Paul's family and friends, the Church community gathers together. Celebrations are an important part of Church life. **Mass** is another name for the celebration of the sacrament of the Eucharist. Since the beginning of the Church, followers of Jesus have come together to worship.

SCRIPTURE Acts 2:42–47

The Community Gathers

After the Holy Spirit came, Jesus' followers met often to learn from the Apostles, to break bread together, and to pray. Some of the members sold what they had and gave the money to help the others. Still others shared their belongings with those who were in need. These followers of Jesus were very happy, and new members joined every day. Based on Acts 2:42–47

- Why do you think the first followers gathered together?
- When does your parish community get together?

The Mass Begins

Every Sunday people wave and greet each other as they walk toward their church. As they enter the church building, greeters say, "Welcome! We are so glad you are here!"

All those gathered together make up the **assembly**. Everyone gathered takes part in the Mass. They sing, pray, and use actions to worship God.

As the Mass begins, the assembly stands. They all sing a gathering song. The altar servers enter carrying a cross in a procession. The readers, deacon, and priest follow. They are singing, too.

Mass is another name for the celebration of the sacrament of the Eucharist.

The **assembly** is the people gathered together for worship.

Activity Share Your Faith

Think: What are some ways you can get ready to take part in the Mass?

Share: Talk about what happens in your home or parish before Mass begins.

Act: Decide one thing you will do to welcome others at Mass next week.

Call on God

How does Mass begin?

After the procession ends, the priest leads everyone in making the Sign of the Cross. He greets everyone, saying, "The Lord be with you." The assembly answers in strong voices, "And with your spirit." These words and actions remind the people that Jesus is present in the priest and people gathered together.

Next the assembly recalls God's forgiveness. The priest asks everyone to think of times they may have hurt others. They ask for God's mercy. They ask God to forgive them for any wrong they have done during the week. They say together,

"Lord, have mercy.
Christ, have mercy.
Lord, have mercy."

What are some ways you can show God's mercy to others?

Words of Praise

With God's forgiveness in your heart, you are better able to pray and take part in the Mass. Many times during the year, the Gloria is sung or prayed during Mass. This is a very old hymn that the Church prays to give praise and honor to God. The hymn begins with these words.

"Glory to God in the highest, and on Earth peace to people of good will."

After this song, the priest invites the people to pray. The priest and assembly are silent for a few moments. The priest then prays the opening prayer, and the people respond "Amen." All gathered are now ready for the first main part of the Mass.

Faith Fact

During the Easter season bells are often rung during the Gloria.

Activity Connect Your Faith

Show the Assembly Draw yourself taking part in the Mass. Label your picture.

Explore

Joining In at Mass

How can you take part in the celebration of the Mass?

The Mass is the great celebration of the followers of Jesus. The priest leads the celebration, but he is not the only person celebrating. The whole assembly gathers to praise and thank God.

You are part of the assembly. You don't go to Mass to watch but to take part in the celebration. Here are some ways you can join in:

- Get to know the parts of the Mass.
- Learn the prayers and responses.
- Arrive on time, ready to participate.
- Greet and be friendly to the other people in the assembly.
- Join in the singing.
- Follow the actions of the priest, deacon, and other ministers.
- Listen to the readings and the homily.
- Show respect in the way you stand, sit, and kneel.

Taking part in the Mass will help you grow closer to Jesus in the Eucharist.

? What things can you do to get ready to celebrate the Mass this week?

Activity — Live Your Faith

Picture Yourself Celebrating In the frame, draw yourself taking part in the Mass with your family and other members of the assembly.

Talk with a Partner Look at the list on page 226. Name the ways to take part in the Mass that you already do well. Share one way you could do better.

Prayer of Praise

Gather and begin with the Sign of the Cross.

Leader: The Lord be with you.

All: **And with your spirit.**

Leader: Sing joyfully to the Lord, all you lands;
serve the Lord with gladness;
come before him with joyful song.

All: **We come to praise you, Lord.**

Leader: Enter his gates with praise,
his courts with thanksgiving.

All: **We come to praise you, Lord.**

Leader: Give thanks to him; bless his name,
for he is good:
The Lord, whose kindness
endures forever.

All: **We come to praise you, Lord. Amen.**

Based on Psalm 100

Sing together the refrain.

We are God's
people,
the flock of
the Lord.

"Psalm 100: We Are God's People" © 1969, 1981, and 1997, ICEL

Review

A Work with Words Circle the correct answer.

1. The ______ is the great celebration of the followers of Jesus.

   Mass **assembly** **procession**

2. At Mass the whole ______ gathers to praise God.

   class **assembly** **neighborhood**

B Check Understanding Use the numbers 1 to 5 to put the actions in the order in which they happen at Mass.

3. ______ The altar servers, deacon, and priest process into the church.
4. ______ The assembly begins to sing the gathering song.
5. ______ The priest says, "The Lord be with you."
6. ______ The assembly gathers.
7. ______ The priest and assembly say, "Lord, have mercy."

C Make Connections Write your answer on the lines.

8-10. Melissa doesn't pay attention at Mass. Name three things she could do to be a part of the assembly at Mass.

____

____

____

Family Faith

Catholics Believe

- Mass is another name for the celebration of the Eucharist.
- The assembly uses songs, prayer, and actions to worship God.

SCRIPTURE

Read Romans 12:3–8 about the different gifts people have to help serve the Lord.

GO online **www.osvcurriculum.com** For weekly scripture readings and seasonal resources

Activity

Live Your Faith

Know the Mass Have each member of your family choose one part from the beginning of the Mass.

- Draw a picture of the part you chose.
- Display the pictures in order.
- Discuss each picture with the family.

▲ Blessed Marguerite Bays, 1815–1879

People of Faith

Blessed Marguerite Bays spent her whole life in the neighborhood where she was born in Switzerland. She was dedicated to the sick and the poor. She called the poor "God's Favorites." At age 35, she became very ill and was miraculously cured. After that, prayer became the focus of her life. She worshipped God in everything that she did.

Family Prayer

God, help us worship you always as Marguerite did. Amen.

In Unit 6 your child is learning about SACRAMENTS.

 CCC *See Catechism of the Catholic Church 1141–1142, 1348 for further reading on chapter content.*

Invite

Chapter 17 Listen to God's Word

Let Us Pray

Leader: Lord, your word gives us hope.
"I wait for longing for the LORD,
my soul waits for his word."
Psalm 130:5

All: Lord, your word gives us hope. Amen.

Activity Let's Begin

Story Time Andrew couldn't wait for story hour at the library. He and his friends always got there early. They wanted to sit up front so they could hear everything. Sometimes they even got to pick out the book. When the reader finished, she would ask questions about the story. Andrew loved to talk about the places and people in the stories.

- What do you like best about reading or listening to stories?

____

____

Talk About Stories In a small group, talk about your favorite story. Tell what the story is about and why you like it.

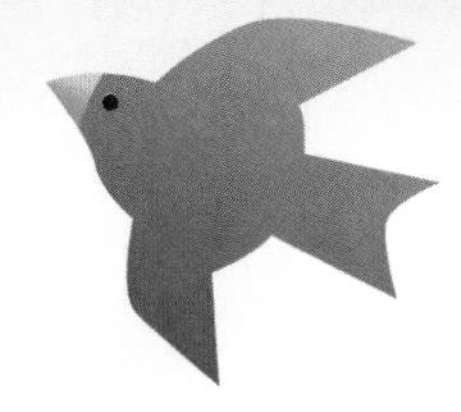

The Liturgy of the Word

Focus **What do you hear at Mass?**

Jesus learned the stories of the Jewish people. He studied Scripture and talked about God's law with wise teachers. Jesus was a wonderful teacher, too. He told many stories.

Some special stories told by Jesus are called parables. **Parables** are short stories about everyday life that help Jesus' followers learn how to love God and to follow him. Here is one parable Jesus told.

SCRIPTURE Matthew 13:31–32

The Mustard Seed

"The kingdom of heaven is like a mustard seed that a person took and sowed in a field. It is the smallest of all the seeds, yet when full grown it is the largest of plants. It becomes a large bush, and the 'birds of the sky come and dwell in its branches.'"

Matthew 13:31–32

Jesus wanted his followers to know that the kingdom would grow with prayer and God's work.

What are some other stories Jesus teaches us?

The Readings Begin

The first main part of the Mass is the **Liturgy of the Word**. The assembly listens to God's word from the Bible. The reader steps forward to proclaim the first reading. It is usually from the Old Testament.

Next, a singer, called a cantor, leads everyone in singing a psalm. Remember, psalms are prayers of praise found in the Old Testament.

Then, either another reader or the same reader stands and reads from one of the letters in the New Testament.

At the end of each reading, the reader says, "The word of the Lord." The assembly answers, "Thanks be to God." After each reading, everyone quietly thinks about what they have heard.

Words of Faith

Parables are short stories about everyday life.

The **Liturgy of the Word** is the first main part of the Mass.

Activity: Share Your Faith

Think: What happens in your parish during the Liturgy of the Word?

Share: Talk about different ways you learn about God's word.

Act: Complete the sentence.

I learn about God's word by ______________________________

____.

The Good News

What makes up the Liturgy of the Word?

Now everyone stands and sings "Alleluia!" It is time to hear the good news of Jesus Christ.

"The Lord be with you," says the priest or deacon. "And with your spirit," the assembly answers.

The priest or deacon announces what Gospel is going to be read. The Gospels contain stories about Jesus, the words of Jesus, and stories that Jesus told. The priest or deacon reads the Good News of Jesus from one of the Gospels.

At the end of the Gospel, the priest or deacon says, "The Gospel of the Lord." Everyone says, "Praise to you, Lord Jesus Christ."

After the reading of the Gospel, the priest gives a homily. The homily is a short talk about the readings. It helps the people gathered understand what it means to follow Jesus.

What Gospel story have you heard recently at Mass?

The People Speak

The assembly then stands to say the **creed** together. You say proudly that you believe in God the Father, God the Son, and God the Holy Spirit. You say that you believe in the Church and its teachings.

Next, the assembly stands together and prays the **Prayer of the Faithful**.

- You pray for the leaders of the Church and of your country.
- You pray for those who are sick and those who have died.
- You pray for people all around the world who have needs at this time.

As a leader says each prayer, you add your answer, such as "Lord, hear our prayer."

Words of Faith

A **creed** is a statement of the Church's beliefs.

The **Prayer of the Faithful** is a prayer at Mass for the needs of the Church and the world.

Activity Connect Your Faith

Write Prayers Think of things that are happening in your family or neighborhood. Who needs your prayers right now? Fill in the blanks in these prayers.

For ______________________, we pray to the Lord.

For ______________________, we pray to the Lord.

Learning from Stories

How did Jesus use stories to teach?

Jesus was a great storyteller. His stories, or parables, used lots of details and characters that were familiar to his listeners. Sometimes his stories had humor to make people laugh or surprise endings to make people think. Best of all, Jesus' stories always had lessons about God's love. Jesus' stories taught people how to show love for God and others and how to be good followers of Jesus. This year you have read or heard some of the parables Jesus told. These are some of them.

The Parable of
The Good Samaritan

Every person is our neighbor. We show love for God when we care for our neighbors in need.

The Parable of
The Forgiving Father

God will always forgive and welcome us when we show that we are sorry for our sins.

The Parable of
The Lost Sheep

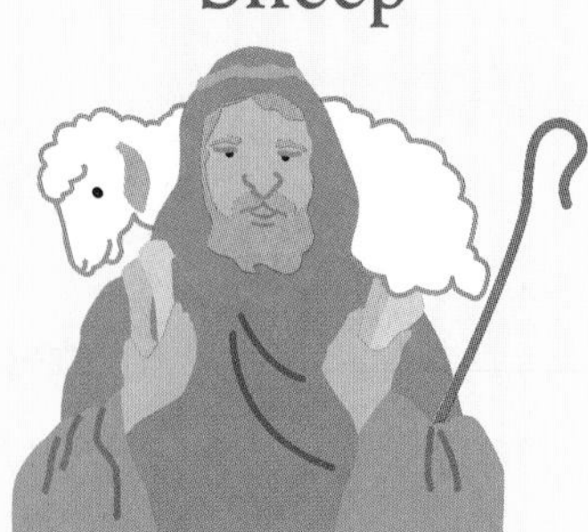

God's love for each person never ends. God will always be with us and care for us.

What is your favorite story Jesus told? Why do you like it?

Activity

Live Your Faith

Act It Out With a small group choose one of Jesus' parables to act out. Use these questions to help you plan your play. Make notes on the lines below to help you remember.

What story will we tell?

Who are the people or the animals in the story?

Who will play which people or animals?

Talk It Over With your group, talk about ways people today can follow the message of this story.

Pray with God's Word

Gather and begin with the Sign of the Cross.

Leader: Gracious God, open our hearts and minds to hear your word.

Reader 1: A reading from the First Letter of John.

Read 1 John 5:13–14.

The word of the Lord.

All: Thanks be to God.

Sing together the refrain.

Alleluia, alleluia, alleluia.

"Alleluia" © 1973, ICEL

Reader 2: A reading from the holy Gospel according to Matthew.

Read Matthew 7:7–8.

The Gospel of the Lord.

All: Praise to you, Lord Jesus Christ.

Review

A Work with Words Match the description in Column 1 with the letter of the correct words in Column 2.

Column 1	Column 2
1. short stories about everyday life that Jesus told _______	**a.** Liturgy of the Word
2. the first part of the Mass _______	**b.** teach
3. Jesus used parables to _______.	**c.** creed
4. a short talk about the readings _______	**d.** parables
5. a statement of the Church's beliefs _______	**e.** homily

B Check Understanding Circle the correct answer.

6. Jesus was a great _______.

storyteller **farmer** **follower**

7. Jesus' stories had lessons about God's _______.

family **friends** **love**

8. God will never stop _______ you.

losing **loving** **scolding**

9. All of Jesus' parables teach you how to _______.

go to Mass **read** **follow Jesus**

C Make Connections Write your answer on the lines.

10. How is the kingdom of God like a mustard seed?

____

____

Family Faith

Catholics Believe

- In the Liturgy of the Word, God's word is read from the Bible.
- We say what we believe about God and pray for the needs of the Church and the world.

SCRIPTURE

Read Matthew 6:32 to learn about how we can count on God.

GO online www.osvcurriculum.com
For weekly scripture readings and seasonal resources

Activity

Live Your Faith

Read God's Word Put a Bible in a place of honor in your home. Place a candle and a crucifix nearby. Place a green plant next to the Bible to show that God's word is the living word. As a family, gather at this place this week and read a story from one of the Gospels. Then offer prayers to God for the needs of your family and friends.

▲ Blessed Mariano de Jesus, 1854–1926

People of Faith

Mariano was born in Colombia, South America. His parents taught him about God and his great love for the world. Even as a child Mariano taught others about God. When he became a priest, people remembered his homilies and his care for people who were poor. Pope Saint John Paul II asked us to follow Father Mariano's example of charity, understanding, and forgiveness. Mariano was beatified in April 2000.

Family Prayer

Blessed Mariano, help us give to those who need our help. May they see God's love through our words and actions. Amen.

In Unit 6 your child is learning about SACRAMENTS.

CCC *See Catechism of the Catholic Church 1154, 1349 for further reading on chapter content.*

Chapter 18

Remember Jesus' Sacrifice

Leader: God, we offer you our thanks and praise.
"I will offer a sacrifice of thanksgiving
and call on the name of the LORD."
Psalm 116:17

All: God, we offer you our thanks and praise. Amen.

Activity Let's Begin

Helping Others When the Twin Towers in New York City burned and fell down in 2001, the children at Tribeca Elementary had nowhere to go to school.

Everybody at Public School #41 wanted to help. It meant they would have to share everything. It wasn't easy, but the students were glad to help.

- If you had been a student at Public School #41, what would you have shared with the students from Tribeca?

____

____

Share a Story With a partner, talk about a time when you were happy that someone shared something with you.

Explore

Thinking of Others

What is the sacrifice Jesus chose to make?

The children at Public School #41 made room in their hearts and in their school. They thought of others before themselves. They made a sacrifice. Sacrifice takes love and courage.

Making a sacrifice can be very difficult. A rich young man found this out when he asked Jesus about life with God forever.

Matthew 19:21–22

The Rich Young Man

Jesus said to him, "If you wish to be perfect, go, sell what you have and give to [the] poor, and you will have treasure in heaven. Then come, follow me."

When the young man heard this . . . , he went away sad, for he had many possessions.

Matthew 19:21–22

The rich young man could not make the sacrifice because he loved his things more than he loved God.

What is a sacrifice you have made for someone?

The Greatest Gift

People make sacrifices, but Jesus chose to make the greatest sacrifice of all. Jesus' sacrifice is that he freely gave up his life on a cross to save all people from the power of sin and everlasting death. He died so that you would have new life with God forever.

God the Father rewarded Jesus for his loving choice. Through God's loving power, Jesus overcame death and was raised to new life.

The Mass is a memorial celebration of Jesus' death and Resurrection. Jesus' great sacrifice is celebrated at every Mass.

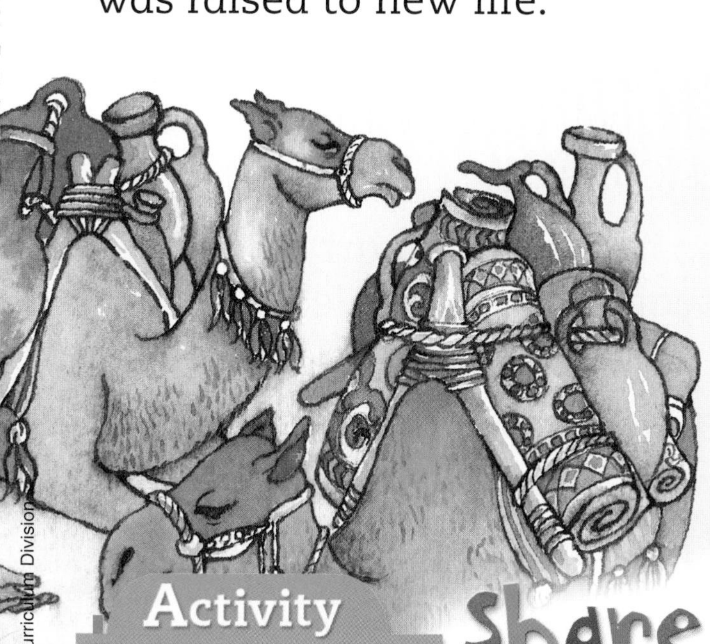

Activity — Share Your Faith

Think: What is a sacrifice you will make for Jesus?

Share: Talk in small groups about sacrifices.

Act: Write about one here.

Give Thanks

Focus What happens to the bread and wine at Mass?

The second main part of the Mass is called the **Liturgy of the Eucharist**. Those gathered remember in a special way Jesus' death and his Resurrection.

Gifts of Bread and Wine

The Liturgy of the Eucharist begins when members of the assembly bring forward the gifts of bread and wine. The people offer these gifts as a sign of their love. The priest prepares the gifts. The bread and wine will become the Body and Blood of Jesus Christ.

Now the most important part of the celebration begins. The priest leads the assembly in prayer.

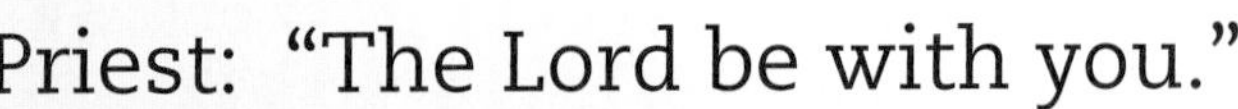

Priest: "The Lord be with you."
All: "And with your spirit."
Priest: "Lift up your hearts."
All: "We lift them up to the Lord."
Priest: "Let us give thanks to the Lord our God."
All: "It is right and just."

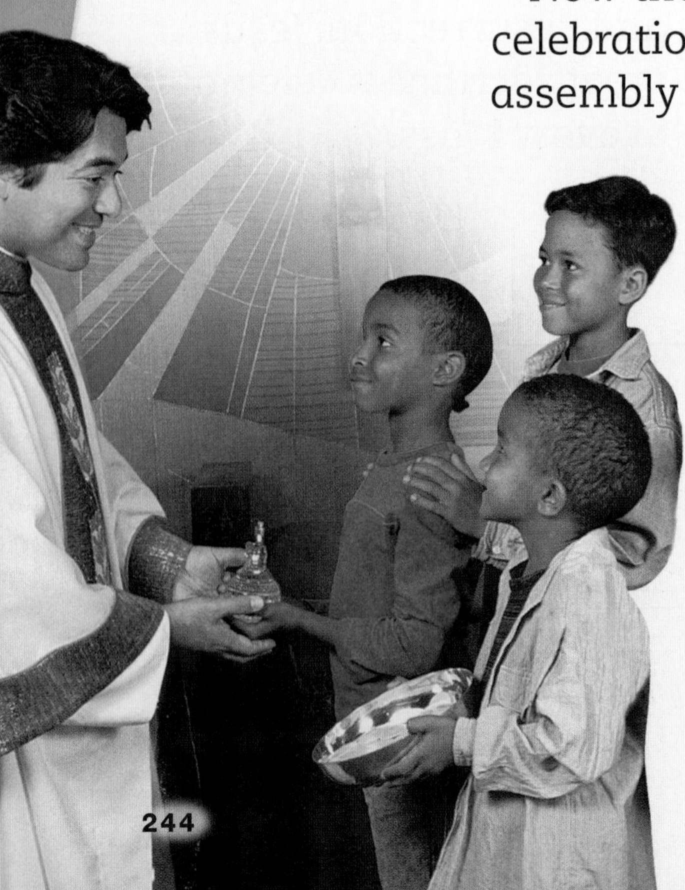

The Eucharistic Prayer

The priest now begins the **Eucharistic Prayer**. He gives thanks and praise to God. He asks the Father to send the Holy Spirit. The priest repeats what Jesus said at the Last Supper:

> "This is my body, which will be given up
> for you . . .
> This is the chalice of my Blood, . . . which will
> be poured out for you and for many
> for the forgiveness of sins.
> Do this in memory of me."

The bread and wine are now the Body and Blood of Christ. The assembly prays:

> "We proclaim your Death, O Lord, and profess your Resurrection until you come again."

The assembly recalls all that Jesus did and offers the Father the gift of his Son. The prayer ends with everyone saying or singing the "Great Amen."

Words of Faith

Liturgy of the Eucharist is the second main part of the Mass.

The **Eucharistic Prayer** is the great prayer of thanksgiving prayed by the priest in your name and that of the Church.

Activity — Connect Your Faith

Find the Word Find the word you say at the end of the Eucharistic Prayer. It means it is true and that you believe in what has happened. Color each X with one color and each O with a different color.

The Mystery of Faith

Focus How do you remember Jesus' sacrifice at Mass?

At Mass, the priest prays the Eucharistic Prayer. He prays for all gathered. The assembly remembers what Jesus said and did at his Last Supper with his friends. The bread and wine become Jesus' own Body and Blood.

Then the priest invites everyone to say aloud what we believe about Jesus' sacrifice. He says to the assembly, "Let us proclaim the mystery of faith." We answer the priest by praying or singing a mystery of faith.

Mysteries of Faith
1. We proclaim your death, O Lord, and profess your Resurrection until you come again.
2. When we eat this Bread and drink this Cup, we proclaim your death, O Lord, until you come again.
3. Save us, Savior of the world, for by your Cross and Resurrection, you have set us free.

The mystery of faith is not a puzzle or a riddle that is hard to solve. It is God's love for us, which is greater than we can ever understand completely. So, we simply say what we believe and thank God in our hearts.

Why should you join in proclaiming the mystery of faith at Mass?

Activity Live Your Faith

Design a Window In many churches, colorful stained glass windows show symbols and pictures that remind us of what we believe. Choose one of the three mysteries of faith from page 246. In the space below, design your own stained glass window. Use symbols or pictures that remind people of this statement of faith.

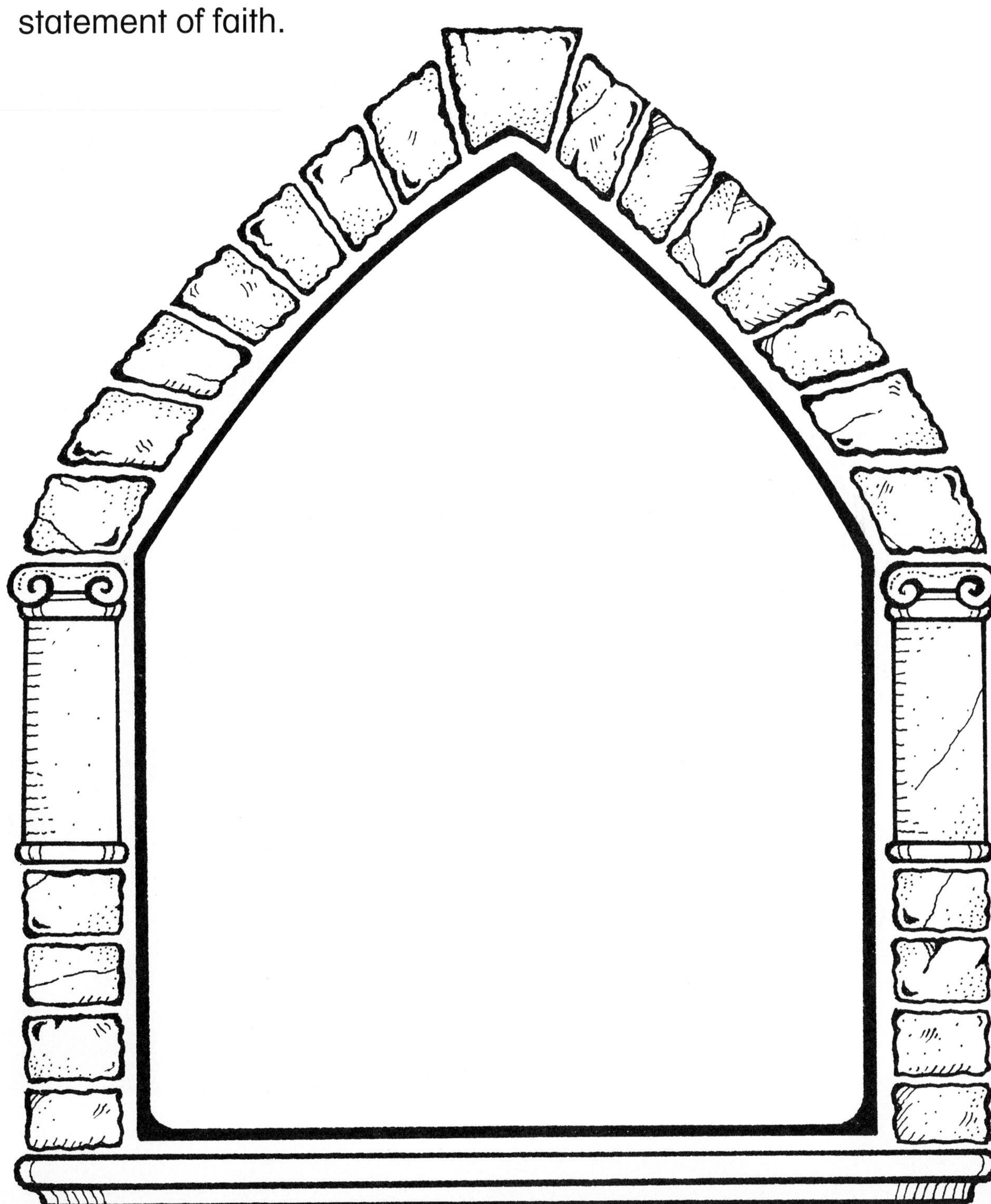

Memorial Prayer

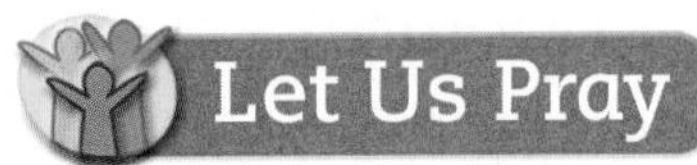

Gather and begin with the Sign of the Cross.

Leader: God our Father, your Son Jesus gave his life for us. Be with us as we pray.

Reader: A reading from the First Letter of Paul to the Corinthians.

Read 1 Corinthians 11:23–26.

The word of the Lord.

All: Thanks be to God.

Sing together.

Amen Siakudmisa.
Amen Siakudmisa.

Amen bawo, Amen bawo,
Amen Siakudmisa.

Amen, we praise your name,
O God.

Amen, we praise your name,
O God.

Amen, sing praise, Amen,
sing praise,

Amen, we praise your name,
O God.

"Amen Siakudmisa/Amen, We Praise Your Name"
South African traditional

Review

A Work with Words Circle the correct answer.

1. Jesus' great _______ was his death on the cross.

   Baptism **sacrifice** **prayer**

2. The _______ become the Body and Blood of Jesus.

   cup and plate **words** **bread and wine**

3. Jesus said, "Do this in _______ of me."

   memory **place** **honor**

4. At the end of the Eucharistic Prayer, the people say, _______.

   Thank you **Amen** **Alleluia**

5. _______ is a memorial of Jesus' death and Resurrection.

   Baptism **Confirmation** **The Mass**

B Check Understanding Draw a line from the description in Column 1 to the correct words in Column 2.

Column A	Column B
6. At Mass, the priest prays the	a. Eucharistic Prayer
7. We remember what Jesus said at	b. God's love for us
8. The second main part of the Mass	c. the Last Supper
9. The mystery of faith is	d. Liturgy of the Eucharist

C Make Connections Write your answer on the line.

10. Why is it important to remember Jesus' sacrifice?

____

____

Family Faith

Catholics Believe

- The Eucharist is a memorial of the sacrifice of Jesus.
- The Liturgy of the Eucharist is the second main part of the Mass.

SCRIPTURE

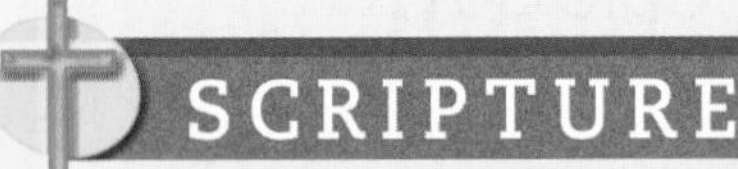

In I Corinthians 11:23–26 Saint Paul writes about the Last Supper.

www.osvcurriculum.com
For weekly scripture readings and seasonal resources

Activity
Live Your Faith

Make Sacrifices Give each person a different color slip of paper. Have all family members write a sacrifice they will make for another family member this week. Put all the papers in a box. As each person makes a sacrifice, he or she can remove their paper from the box.

▲ Saint Pius X (Giuseppe Sarto), 1835–1914

People of Faith

Giuseppe Sarto was born in Italy. He became a priest and a teacher of young men studying to be priests. In 1903 he was elected pope. He is known as the Pope of the Blessed Sacrament. He wanted young children to receive Communion daily if possible. Pope Pius X promoted Gregorian chant, which is beautiful Church music. He asked priests to give clear and simple homilies at Mass. The Church celebrates his feast day on August 21.

Family Prayer

Saint Pius X, pray to God for us that we may receive Holy Communion with reverence. Amen.

In Unit 6 your child is learning about KINGDOM OF GOD.

 CCC *See Catechism of the Catholic Church 1356–1358 for further reading on chapter content.*

DISCOVER

Catholic Social Teaching:

Call to Family, Community, and Participation

In this unit you learned that all are welcomed at Mass. The parish community gathers to celebrate Jesus' gift of himself. It is important to take part in Mass.

Get Involved!

God made people to live in families and communities. People need other people to share God's love. You are part of your own family, and part of the family of all God's people. You are part of many communities—your neighborhood, your school, your parish, and the Church around the world.

It is good to know that you are not alone. The gifts of family and community come with responsibilities, too. God calls everyone to take part in family and community. We need to help others so no one is left out, and no one feels alone.

What is one way you are involved in your family and one way you are involved in a community?

CONNECT

With the Call to Justice

Making Room

Everyone is called to get involved in family life and community life. Let's see how the members of one parish community are reaching out to those who feel alone.

Do you remember the Christmas story? Jesus was born in a shelter for animals, because there was no room at the inn.

Every year in wintertime, homeless people must feel the way Mary and Joseph did—alone, cold, and left out. There are often many more homeless people living on the streets than there are places for them to stay. In Tennessee, a Catholic priest saw homeless people sleeping outside in the cold. He thought about Mary and Joseph. So he started a program called Room in the Inn. In the winter, churches welcome homeless people to sleep on church property, and they give them meals.

? How does the Room in the Inn program help homeless people?

Reach Out!

SERVE

Your Community

Make a List

Name three ways you take part in the life of your family and your community. With a partner, name three ways your class could take part.

Ways I Take Part	Ways the Class Takes Part
1.	1.
2.	2.
3.	3.

Make a Difference

Help Your Community Find out what helpful events your community has planned. Work as a class to help—for example, by raising money for walkers or runners, baking cookies for a bake sale, helping to wash cars, or making signs. Invite other classes to join you.

Unit 6 Review

A **Work with Words** Complete each sentence with the correct word from the Word Bank.

WORD BANK

Eucharist
Word
assembly
Mass
creed

1. ________________ is another name for the celebration of the Sacrament of the Eucharist.

2. In the Liturgy of the ________________, stories from the Bible are read.

3. The ________________ is the people gathered together for worship.

4. The Liturgy of the ________________ is the second main part of the Mass.

5. A ________________ is a statement of the Church's beliefs.

B **Check Understanding** Match the description in Column I with the letter of the correct words in Column 2.

Column I	Column 2
6. what the assembly says at the end of the Eucharistic Prayer ______	a. Jesus' sacrifice
7. when the bread and wine become the Body and Blood of Christ ______	b. homily
8. a talk about Scripture readings ______	c. "Great Amen"
9. the priest or deacon reads this ______	d. Eucharistic Prayer
10. each Mass celebrates this ______	e. the Gospel

Circle **T** if the sentence is TRUE. Circle **F** if the sentence is FALSE.

11. The priest leads the assembly in celebrating the Mass. **T F**
12. At Mass you do not take part in the celebration. **T F**
13. Jesus' stories are called parables. **T F**
14. Jesus' parables teach us about God's love. **T F**
15. The Mass is a memorial celebration of Jesus' birth and life. **T F**

C **Make Connections** The Mass is a holy meal. How is the Mass like a family meal? Write about parts of the Mass that remind you of parts of a family meal.

16. Your cousins come for Sunday dinner.
17. Your family welcomes everyone to the table.
18. Family members tell stories during the meal.
19. Family members bring food and drink to share.
20. Your family shares a meal of food and drink.

Unit 7
Kingdom of God

In this unit you will...

learn that God wants us to be one with him. The Eucharist unites us with Jesus and with one another. Because we are united, we share the same mission to love the way Jesus did. We spread the news of the kingdom of God to everyone. The Eucharist is a sign of what heaven will be like— happiness forever with God.

Faith in Action!

Catholic Social Teaching Principle: Option for the Poor and Vulnerable

Chapter 19 Share a Holy Meal

Let Us Pray

Leader: Thank you, God, for giving us what we need.

"Let the faithful rejoice in their glory,
cry out for joy at their banquet."

Psalm 149:5

All: Thank you, God, for giving us what we need. Amen.

Activity Let's Begin

Antonio's Feast Antonio lived on the eighth floor of an apartment building. He had the measles. His mother's friend Mrs. Johnson lived on the first floor. She made his favorite soup and climbed the stairs to take it to him.

"Everyone I passed wanted to send something along, Antonio," she said. Peeking into her basket, Antonio saw bread, olives, cheese, apples, and flowers. When he saw these things, his heart was full.

- Why did seeing the things in Mrs. Johnson's basket make Antonio happy?

____

____

Draw a Feast Think of the kinds of things you would want someone to share with you. Draw a basket filled with these good things.

Prepare the Meal

Focus How did Jesus share food with others?

Jesus knew how important food was for life. The Gospels have many stories of Jesus sharing meals with his friends.

SCRIPTURE Luke 9:10-17

The Loaves and Fishes

One day Jesus was speaking to a crowd of five thousand people. Late in the day, the Apostles told Jesus to send the crowds away to nearby villages to find food.

Jesus told the Apostles to feed the people themselves. "How can we do that?" they asked. "We have only five loaves of bread and two fish."

Jesus told them to have the people sit down. He took the bread and fish, looked up to heaven, and blessed the food. He broke it into pieces and gave the pieces to his followers to pass out among the people.

Everyone had enough to eat. The leftovers filled twelve straw baskets.

Based on Luke 9:10–17

How did Jesus take care of the people?

The Lord's Prayer

Jesus continues to feed his followers. In the Mass Jesus gives you his Body and Blood. After the assembly sings the Great Amen at Mass, it is time to prepare for a holy meal. The meal is **holy** because the bread and wine have become the Body and Blood of Christ.

The assembly stands to say or sing the Lord's Prayer. When you pray the Lord's Prayer, you pray that God will help you be more like him and you show your trust in God for all you need.

After the Lord's Prayer, those gathered offer the peace of Christ to one another. This is a sign of love and a reminder that all are united by Jesus' love.

Words of Faith

Something that is **holy** is from God or shows what God is like.

Activity Share Your Faith

Think: What are some ways children your age can trust in God?

Share: Break into two groups and talk about it.

Act: Write ways you will trust in God today.

Remember Jesus

Focus **What happens in Mass after the Lord's Prayer?**

When Jesus shared the bread and fish with the hungry people, they felt Jesus' love and care. At Mass, Jesus' followers remember Jesus' love for them as they share in his Body and Blood.

Holy Communion

After the sign of peace, the priest breaks the holy Bread before he eats it and shares it. This is what Jesus did at the Last Supper. The priest's action again reminds the assembly that Jesus died and was raised from the dead for all people.

The Body and Blood of Christ that you will receive is called **Holy Communion**. If you are free from serious sin, you are welcome at the Lord's table. When you receive Holy Communion, you are one with Jesus and all his Church.

What do you remember at Mass?

The Body of Christ

The Body and Blood of Jesus is a great gift. When you receive it, you show **reverence**, or care and respect.

You walk to the altar prayerfully. The priest, deacon, or an extraordinary minister of the Holy Communion says, "The Body of Christ," and you say, "Amen." You receive the Body of Christ in your hand or on your tongue. You may also receive the Blood of Christ from the cup.

After you receive Holy Communion, you go back to your place and sing with everyone. Then you pray in silence.

The priest then prays the final prayer. He asks God's blessing on all gathered and sends everyone out to continue Jesus' work.

Words of Faith

Holy Communion is holy Bread and Wine that you receive in the Eucharist.

Reverence is the care and respect you show to God and holy persons and things.

Activity Connect Your Faith

Show Reverence Draw one action at Mass that shows respect and care. Label the action.

Explore

The Blessed Sacrament

Focus **How do we honor Jesus in the Eucharist outside the Mass?**

Some people cannot join the community at Mass. They may be sick at home or in the hospital. Some elderly people are too weak to travel. All these people are still a part of the assembly. They are still joined to the community in prayer. After Mass they may be visited by the priest, a deacon, or an extraordinary minister of Holy Communion who brings Holy Communion to them and prays with them.

Any other Hosts reserved, or left over, after Mass are stored in a beautiful cabinet or container called the *tabernacle*. Jesus remains present in the reserved Hosts, also called the Blessed Sacrament. A lamp always burns in front of the tabernacle to remind people that Jesus is present.

Outside of Mass, people are usually welcome to visit the church and spend some time in prayer before the tabernacle.

? How can you respect Jesus' presence in the Eucharist?

Activity

Live Your Faith

Make a Card Those who cannot participate in Mass are still part of the community. They are joined by prayer and the care of the parish community. Write and decorate the prayer card below for parish members who cannot be present at Mass.

Celebrate

Pray with God's Word

Gather and begin at the Sign of the Cross.

Leader: The Lord be with you.

All: And with your spirit.

Leader: Let us pray.

Bow your heads as the leader prays.

All: Amen.

Reader: A reading from the First Letter of Paul to the Corinthians.

Read 1 Corinthians 10:16–17.

The word of the Lord.

All: Thanks be to God.

Sing together the refrain.

I am the church! You are the church!
We are the church together!
All who follow Jesus,
all around the world!
Yes, we're the
church together!

Review

A Work with Words Use the words from the Word Bank to complete the sentences.

WORD BANK

- Reverence
- Holy Communion
- Blessed Sacrament
- holy

1. Something that is ______________ is from God or shows what God is like.

2. ______________________ is the holy Bread and Wine.

3. ________________ is the care and respect you show to God and holy persons and things.

4. The ______________________ is the name we give to the hosts kept in the tabernacle.

B Check Understanding Use the numbers 1 to 5 to put the actions in the order in which they happen at Mass.

5. ________ The priest breaks the bread.

6. ________ All gather to pray the Lord's Prayer.

7. ________ The priest sends the assembly out to love and serve the Lord.

8. ________ The people offer the sign of peace.

9. ________ The people receive Holy Communion.

10. Why is it important to show reverence when you receive Holy Communion?

____

Family Faith

Catholics Believe

- Through the Eucharist, Jesus' followers are united with him and one another.
- The gift of Holy Communion is received with reverence.

SCRIPTURE

Read Romans 12:9–15 to learn how to love and serve the Lord.

www.osvcurriculum.com
For weekly scripture readings and seasonal resources

Activity

Live Your Faith

Keep the Fast Fasting is a way to show respect and reverence for Christ in the Eucharist. The Eucharistic fast requires you not to eat or drink (except water) for an hour before you receive Holy Communion. Make a reminder poster to hang in the kitchen so that all will remember to keep the fast before Mass.

People of Faith

▲ Saint Tarsicius, third or fourth century A.D.

Tarsicius moved through Rome on a secret mission. He carried the holy Bread of the Eucharist to Christians who were in prison because of their faith in Jesus. Some people who were not Christians discovered his secret mission. They began to throw stones at him. The story of Tarsicius reminds all Catholics to respect the presence of Jesus in the Eucharist. Saint Tarsicius is the patron saint of altar servers. His feast day is August 26.

Family Prayer

Saint Tarsicius, pray for us that we may help others see the presence of Jesus in the Eucharist. Amen.

In Unit 7 your child is learning about the KINGDOM OF GOD.

CCC *See Catechism of the Catholic Church 1391–1392 for further reading on chapter content.*

Chapter 20 Go Forth!

Let Us Pray

Leader: Lord, we want to do your work.
"Teach me to do your will,
for you are my God.
May your kind spirit guide me."
Psalm 143:10

All: Lord, we want to do your work. Amen.

Activity Let's Begin

Good News Gazette

"Brother and Sister Stop Fighting"
"Girl Obeys Her Parents All Week"
"Second Graders Clean Up City Garden"
"No Crime in Town Last Night"
"World at Peace"
"Family Helps Poor"

- What good news have you heard today?

____

____

Make a List Write down some good things you did this week. With a partner, talk about how your good deeds helped others.

Explore

Share the Good News

Focus **How can you take part in the mission of the Church?**

At the end of Mass, the priest tells you to go in peace. You leave to share God's good news. Jesus' first followers took his good news to people everywhere.

SCRIPTURE **Acts 10:42–48**

Peter Preaches

Peter told the people of Jerusalem that Jesus sent the apostles to preach to all people.

The apostles shared the good news about God the Father, Jesus, the Son of God, and the Holy Spirit. Peter told the people that Jesus wanted everyone to believe in him. If they believed, they would receive forgiveness through Jesus' name.

After listening to Peter, many people from faraway places asked to be baptized. Peter told the crowd that anyone who was moved by the Spirit could be baptized.

Based on Acts 10:42–48

What are some things Peter might have told the people?

The Church's Mission

Peter and the other Apostles shared Jesus' good news. Today the Church's work is to share the good news of Jesus and God's kingdom throughout the world. This work is called the Church's **mission**. All its members share in this mission.

Most Church members share Jesus' message right where they are. Others bring the message of Jesus to faraway places. They are called **missionaries**.

Words of Faith

Mission is the work of the Church.

Missionaries are people who bring the good news of Jesus and God's kingdom to people in other places.

Activity Share Your Faith

Think: What can you do to bring Jesus' message of love to others?

Share: With a partner complete this chart.

Jesus Teaches	What You Can Do
Encourage those who are afraid.	
Help those who are weak.	
Be patient with all.	

Act: By your actions this week, share the message of love.

Called to Love and Serve

Focus How did Mother Cabrini share Jesus' message?

Different people work to spread Jesus' message in different ways. Not everyone has the same gifts, but everyone can share Jesus' love.

BIOGRAPHY

A Message of Love

In 1850 in a small village in Italy, Frances Xavier Cabrini was born. She was the youngest of thirteen children. Frances was sickly throughout her life, but this did not stop her from doing God's work.

Her parents read aloud the lives of the saints. Hearing the stories, Frances wanted to be a missionary in China, if God willed. Frances wanted to be a religious sister, but no group wanted her because she was sickly. So she founded her own community, the Missionary Sisters of the Sacred Heart.

Why did Frances Cabrini start her own community of sisters?

Curriculum Division

Pope Leo XIII suggested that Frances go to the United States to help Italian immigrants there. Although she had a great fear of water, she crossed the ocean to New York. There she set up a home for orphaned Italian girls and other services for those who were poor.

By the time she was sixty-seven years old, Frances had set up over sixty schools, hospitals, orphanages, and convents throughout the world. In 1917 she died.

In 1946 Frances became the first United States citizen to be named a saint of the Catholic Church. She had carried out the Church's mission, bringing the love of Jesus to those in need.

Connect Your Faith

Spread the Good News You can help spread Jesus' good news. Circle two things that you will do during the next week.

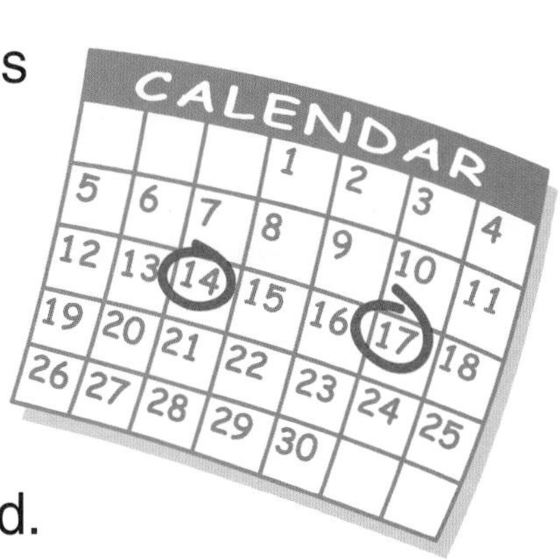

- Share your time or talent with someone who needs help.
- Pray for missionaries.
- Stand up for someone who needs a friend.
- Pray for someone who has hurt you.
- Tell someone you hurt that you are sorry.

Explore

Guides for the Journey

Who can help you learn about Jesus?

Learning about Jesus is like a journey that lasts your whole life. There is always more to learn. It's a good thing there are many people who can help you keep learning. They are your guides on the journey.

Here are some people in your parish who can help you keep growing in faith.

Person	How He or She Helps
Priest	Celebrates Mass and the sacraments Gives homilies to help people understand the Bible
Deacon	Proclaims the Gospel at Mass Helps those who are sick or in need
Eucharistic minister	Helps give Holy Communion at Mass Brings Holy Communion to people who cannot attend Mass
Catechist or religion teacher	Teaches children and adults about Jesus Prepares children to receive the sacraments
Director of religious education	Plans programs for everyone who wants to learn more about Jesus
School Principal	Helps make your school a place where students can come to know Jesus

One important person is missing from this list—you! Jesus sends you on a mission to teach other people about God's love.

What is one way you can teach people about God's love this week?

Activity

Live Your Faith

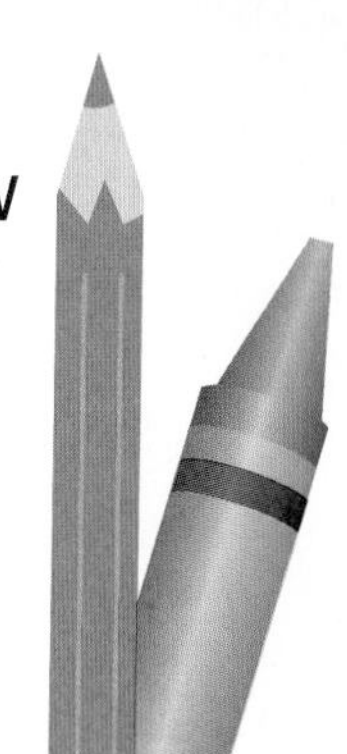

Make a Thank-You Card Think of someone you know who teaches people about Jesus. Make a thank-you card for that person. Use these spaces to plan your card.

In the space below, draw or write what you want to show on the front of the card.

In the space above, write the message for the inside of the card.

Blessing Prayer

Gather and begin with the Sign of the Cross.

Leader: Make a Sign of the Cross on your forehead. May you always remember to follow Jesus.

All: Amen.

Leader: Make a Sign of the Cross over your closed eyes. May you learn to see Jesus in all whom you meet.

All: Amen.

Leader: Make a Sign of the Cross on your lips. May all your words show respect.

All: Amen.

Leader: Make a Sign of the Cross over your heart. May love move you to action and may God give you strength to carry on the work of Jesus.

All: Amen.

Sing together.

May God bless and keep us, may God smile on us.
May God show us kindness, fill us with peace.
And may God bless us, Father, Son, and Spirit;
May we always love and serve, filled with God's peace.

Review

A **Work with Words** Write the letter of the correct words from the Word Bank to complete each sentence.

WORD BANK

a. mission
b. Frances Cabrini
c. missionary
d. Church
e. good news

1. ______ was a missionary who worked in the United States.
2. Jesus' message of God's saving love is called the ______.
3. The Church's ______ is to share the good news of Jesus and God's kingdom.
4. A ______ is a person sent to carry the good news of Jesus to people in faraway places.
5. All the members of the ______ share in its mission.

B **Check Understanding** Draw a line from the names in Column A to the correct descriptions in Column B.

Column A	Column B
6. priest	a. proclaims the Gospel at Mass
7. Catechist	b. celebrates Mass and the sacraments
8. deacon	c. helps make school a place where students can come to know Jesus
9. school principal	d. teaches about Jesus

C **Make Connections** Write your answer on the lines.

10. What is the Church's mission?

____

____

Family Faith

Catholics Believe

- The Church's mission is to share Jesus' message of love and to spread the news of the kingdom of God.
- All members of the Church share in its mission.

SCRIPTURE

Acts 1:8 tells about the Apostles' mission.

www.osvcurriculum.com
For weekly scripture readings and seasonal resources

Activity

Live Your Faith

Serve Others' Needs As a family, look in the bulletin for the names of people who serve the needs of your parish. Also look for ways that the parish community carries on Jesus' mission by serving the needs of people in your local area. Make an action plan for taking part in your parish's service activities.

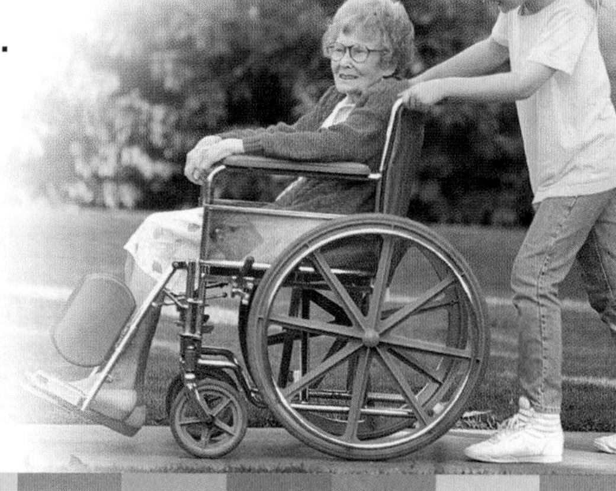

▲ Saint Anthony Claret, 1801–1870

People of Faith

Anthony was born in Spain. His father taught him to weave and make designs. He also learned how to print books. Later, Anthony became a priest and then a bishop. He was a missionary in Cuba for seven years. He used all of his skills to lead people to Jesus. To be sure that his work would continue after his death, he started an order of priests, the Claretians. He also started a company that printed religious books. Saint Anthony's feast day is October 24.

Family Prayer

Saint Anthony, pray for us that we may use our skills to teach others about Jesus. Amen.

In Unit 7 your child is learning about the KINGDOM OF GOD.
CCC See Catechism of the Catholic Church 900–905 for further reading on chapter content.

Chapter 21

Forever in Heaven

Invite

Let Us Pray

Leader: God, we want to be with you forever.
"You set a table before me . . .
my cup overflows." Psalm 23:5

All: God, we want to be with you forever. Amen.

Activity Let's Begin

A Family Picnic The gathering had been nearly perfect. All the cousins were there and lots of friends, too.

The twins spent the afternoon swimming and playing. Later, everyone joined together for games. At supper the tables were loaded with all kinds of food. It was a real feast.

"Let's get the car packed up, kids," said Dad.

"Can't we stay longer?" said Jill.

"How much longer?" asked Dad.

"How about forever?" said Jesse.

- Why do you think Jesse wanted the picnic to last forever?

Draw a Wonderful Day Think of a day that you wanted to last forever. Draw a picture of that time.

Explore

All Are Welcome

To what does God invite you?

Heaven is life and happiness forever with God.

Jesse wanted the party to go on forever. God the Father invites everyone to the happiness of his great love in **heaven** forever. Jesus told this story to help people understand that God the Father wants everyone to enjoy this happiness.

SCRIPTURE Matthew 22:2–10 and Luke 14:15–23

The Wedding Feast

Storyteller: A king gave a wedding feast for his son. When everything was ready, the king sent his servants out to invite the guests.

Servants: The feast is ready. It's time to come and celebrate.

Three people: We can't come. We have a lot of work to do. We are very busy.

Storyteller: The servant brought this message home to the king.

What do you think the king will say? What will he do?

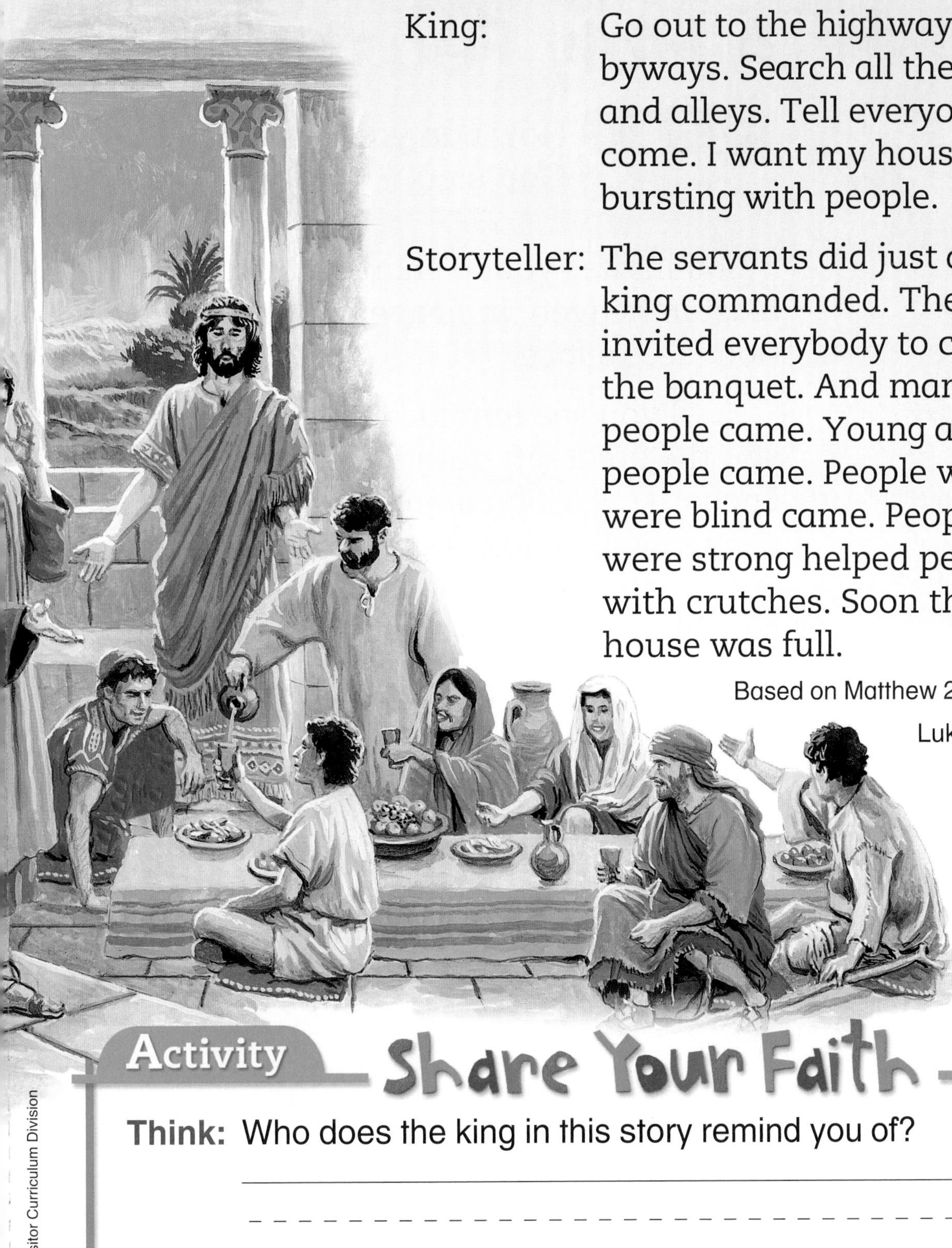

King: Go out to the highways and byways. Search all the paths and alleys. Tell everyone to come. I want my house bursting with people.

Storyteller: The servants did just as the king commanded. They invited everybody to come to the banquet. And many people came. Young and old people came. People who were blind came. People who were strong helped people with crutches. Soon the house was full.

Based on Matthew 22:2–10 and Luke 14:15–23

Activity Share Your Faith

Think: Who does the king in this story remind you of?

____

Who do the invited guests remind you of?

____

Share: With a partner share your answers.

Act: Break into two groups and act out the Bible story.

A Holy Feast

Focus How can you answer God's call?

God invites you to share in the great feast in heaven. In heaven you will see God face to face.

Until you see him face to face, God gives you the great gift of the Eucharist. The Eucharist is a sign of joy and of what heaven will be like. Receiving the Eucharist helps you look forward to the day when you will be with God in heaven.

Every time you receive Holy Communion, you receive the food that helps you live forever in Jesus Christ.

Why do you think the Eucharist is a reminder of heaven?

Faith Fact

God made angels to be with him in heaven and to be his messengers.

Say "Yes" to God!

God calls you to know, love, and serve him. You are like the guests in the Bible story. God invites you to share in a great feast. You can refuse to come. Or you can joyfully accept.

God invites you to say "yes" each day. Here are some ways you say "yes" to God.

- Obey the law of love.
- Listen to God's word in the Bible.
- Take part in Mass and receive Holy Communion.
- Seek God's forgiveness in the Sacrament of Reconciliation.
- Forgive and love other people.
- Help people in need.
- Pray to God each day.

Activity

Connect Your Faith

Answering God's Call
Living a Christian life means answering God's loving call every day. Make a list of things you do each day to say "yes" to God's invitation.

Saying "Yes" to God

What can you learn from Mary about showing love for God?

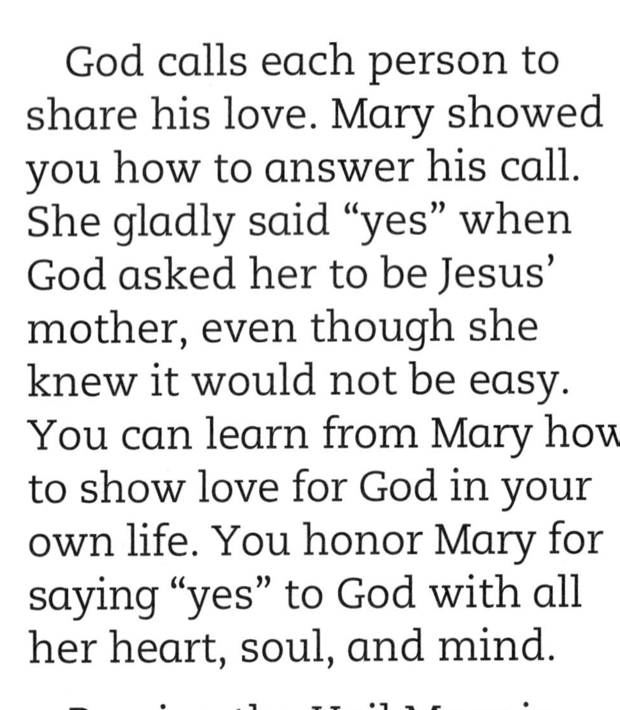

God calls each person to share his love. Mary showed you how to answer his call. She gladly said "yes" when God asked her to be Jesus' mother, even though she knew it would not be easy. You can learn from Mary how to show love for God in your own life. You honor Mary for saying "yes" to God with all her heart, soul, and mind.

Praying the Hail Mary is a way to honor Mary.

Words of the Prayer	What They Mean
Hail, Mary, full of grace.	Mary, you are filled with God's love.
The Lord is with you.	You are very close to God.
Blessed are you among women,	God has chosen you for an important mission.
and blessed is the fruit of your womb, Jesus.	The baby growing inside you is very special.
Holy Mary, Mother of God,	Your child is the Son of God!
pray for us sinners	Please pray for us, because we don't always say "yes" to God, as you did.
now and at the hour of our death.	Be with us all through our lives.
Amen.	Yes, we believe this!

? What is one way you can say "yes" to God today?

Activity

Live Your Faith

Write a Story Think about a time when you or someone you know said "yes" to God, as Mary did. Write a story about it on the lines below.

Share Your Story Read or tell your story to a partner.

Pray with God's Word

Gather and begin with the Sign of the Cross.

Leader: We rejoice that God invites us to heaven. He sent Jesus to show us the way.

Reader: A reading from the holy Gospel according to John.

Read John 3:16.

The Gospel of the Lord.

All: Praise to you, Lord Jesus Christ.

Leader: Let us pray.

Bow your heads as the leader prays.

All: Amen.

Leader: Go forth and share God's love with one another.

All: Thanks be to God.

Sing together.

Glory and gratitude and praise
now let earth to heaven raise.
Glory and gratitude and praise:
these we offer to God.

Review

A Work with Words Fill in the blank with the correct word from the Word Bank.

WORD BANK

feast
happy
Eucharist
serve

1. God wants people to be ______________.

2. God calls us to ______________.

3. The ______________ is a sign of the joy of heaven.

4. The kingdom of heaven is like a ______________.

B Check Understanding Circle **T** if the sentence is TRUE. Circle **F** if the sentence if FALSE.

5. Heaven is life and happiness forever with God. **T F**
6. God calls only very holy people to share his love. **T F**
7. Mary gladly said "yes" to God's call to be the mother of his Son, Jesus. **T F**
8. You honor Mary when you show love for God in your own life. **T F**
9. Praying the Lord's Prayer is a way to honor Mary. **T F**

C Make Connections Write your answers on the line.

10. Your mother asks you to clean your room. Your friends want you to play. How can you say "yes" to God?

____

Family Faith

Catholics Believe

- Heaven is life and happiness forever with God.
- The Eucharist is a sign of joy and of what heaven will be like.

SCRIPTURE

Read John 17:3–5 to find out what Jesus says about life forever with God.

www.osvcurriculum.com
For weekly scripture readings and seasonal resources

Activity

Live Your Faith

Spread the Message "Where charity and love are, there is God," is the line of an ancient Christian hymn. Spread some charity at home. Arrange a surprise message for one another. The message, which might be found in a lunch bag or on a pillow, might say, "Thanks for sharing your things. I like being your sister (or brother)."

▲ All Saints

People of Faith

Saints are people who put God first in their lives. They are reminders that God is calling each person to friendship and happiness with him forever. Saints chose to say "yes" to God. They chose to love and serve as Jesus did. Some saints were children. Others lived to a very old age. All the saints in heaven now see God face to face. November 1 is the feast of All Saints. On this day, Catholics remember all who are alive with God forever.

Family Prayer

All you holy saints, pray for us to God. Ask him to show us the ways of love. Amen.

In Unit 7 your child is learning about the KINGDOM OF GOD.

CCC See Catechism of the Catholic Church 1023–1030 for further reading on chapter content.

DISCOVER

Catholic Social Teaching:

Option for the Poor and Vulnerable

Faith in Action!

CATHOLIC SOCIAL TEACHING

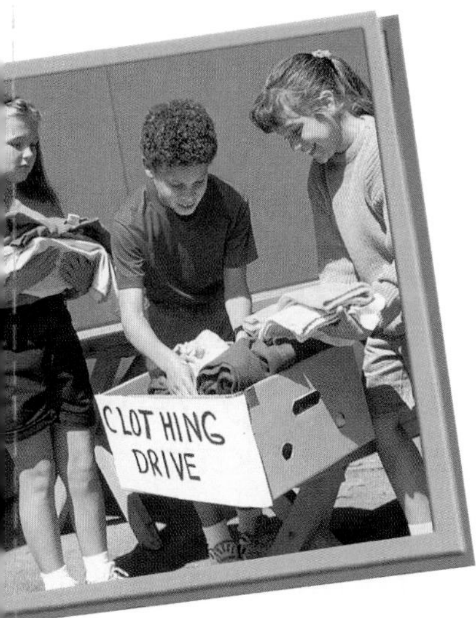

In this unit you learned that Mass is a holy meal. You will spend your whole life learning to know Jesus better and following him more closely. You say "yes" to God when you reach out to others.

Those Most in Need

One day Jesus was talking with his disciples. They asked him how they could follow him more closely. Jesus told them, "Whatever you do for your brothers and sisters who are most in need, you do for me. When you care for them, you care for me. When you turn your back on them, you turn your back on me." (Based on Matthew 25:31–46)

Jesus asks us to use the same message. "Look for those who need your care the most," Jesus says. "When you reach out to help them, you will find me."

Who are the people in your community who are most in need?

CONNECT

With the Call to Justice

WITH A LITTLE HELP

Jesus asks us to look for his face in everyone we meet, especially those most in need. Let's look at how one group of students saw Jesus in the faces of people who do not have a home.

Some people do not have a place to live. They are homeless. People become homeless for many reasons. They can be men, women, or even families. Some things are not easy to do without a place to call home. People who are homeless have a hard time staying warm when it is cold outside. They often visit places, called shelters, to eat and get warm.

Holy Family Catholic School is in Dale City, Virginia. Some students at this school help homeless people stay warm. Every year around Thanksgiving, these students knit scarves for the homeless. Their teacher, Ms. Creed, shows them how to make the clothing. They use a tool called a loom. It takes a few weeks to finish the scarves. The students donate the scarves to a nearby homeless shelter.

About fifty people come to the homeless shelter each day. The Holy Family students make about twenty-five scarves for the people who need them. Ms. Creed said it is a simple way to help. One student named Megan said she enjoys knowing that she has helped someone, even just a little. Another student named Vera said she likes making the scarves because it feels good to help other people.

How did the students at Holy Family Catholic School reach out to others?

Responses will vary.

Reach Out!

Make a Collage

Now it is your turn to look for the face of Jesus in those who are in need. Copy or cut out a picture of Jesus. Glue the picture to a poster board. Then look through old magazines for pictures of people who are in need, or people who are helping others. Cut out the pictures and glue them around the face of Jesus.

Hang your finished poster at home to remind you to look for Jesus in others.

Make a Difference

Pack Your Bags Work together as a class to pack lunches for children in a local daycare center or family shelter. Or fill plastic food storage bags with personal items, such as washcloths, toothbrushes, toothpaste, and soap, or school supplies. Send the bags to a place that helps children in need.

Unit 7 Review

A Work with Words Complete each sentence with the letter of the correct word from the Word Bank.

WORD BANK

a. heaven
b. holy
c. serve
d. mission
e. Reverence

1. Something that is from God is ______.
2. ______ is the care and respect you show to God and holy things.
3. A ______ is the work the Church is sent to do.
4. God wants you to be with him forever in ______.
5. God calls you to know, love, and ______ him.

B Check Understanding Circle the correct answer.

6. A person who brings the good news of Jesus to people in other places is a ______.

   missionary **priest** **teacher**

7. The Body of Christ received at Mass is ______.

   wine **Holy Communion** **a mission**

8. The first American saint was ______.

   Frances Cabrini **Saint Peter** **Pope Leo XIII**

9. When you receive Holy Communion, you are ______.

   a missionary **a priest** **one with the Church**

10. Jesus teaches that heaven is like a great ______.

    feast **fish** **Church**

Unscramble the words to complete each sentence.

11. Hosts left over in the tabernacle at church are called the Blessed CRAMENSAT.

12. People at home or in the hospital are still joined to the community in YAERPR.

13. After Mass, these people may be visited by a priest, a deacon, or an extraordinary minister of Holy Communion who brings the HUISECTRA.

C **Make Connections** Circle **T** if the sentence is TRUE. Circle **F** if the sentence is FALSE.

14. Learning about Jesus is like a journey that lasts your whole life. **T F**
15. The people who help us learn more about Jesus are called guides. **T F**
16. Jesus sends you on a mission to teach other people about yourself. **T F**
17. Mary always said "yes" to God. **T F**
18. Praying the Our Father is one way you can honor Mary. **T F**
19. You can learn from Mary how to show love for God. **T F**
20. God calls only priests and missionaries to share his love. **T F**

Catholic Source Book

Scripture

The Bible

The **Bible** is God's word to people. It is one great book, made up of many small books. The word Bible means "books." Another name for the Bible is Scripture, which means "writing." The Bible has two parts.

The Old Testament

The Old Testament is the largest part of the Bible. It tells of God's love for people, especially the Jewish people, before the coming of Jesus.

The New Testament

This part tells of God's love for people after the coming of Jesus. The New Testament contains four main sections. The first section is the Gospels. The word gospel means "good news." The Gospels tell of the good news that the early Christians believed about Jesus and the kingdom of God. They are:

- The Gospel according to Matthew
- The Gospel according to Mark
- The Gospel according to Luke
- The Gospel according to John

Faith Fact

The Gospel according to Mark was the first Gospel written. It is also the shortest Gospel.

Parables

The Gospels contain stories about Jesus, the words of Jesus, words other people said about Jesus, and stories that Jesus told.

Some special stories told by Jesus are called **parables**. Parables are short stories that help people better understand a truth or mystery about God. For example, to help people better understand how much God loves all people and wants them to be happy with him forever, Jesus told the parables of the Good Shepherd, the Good Samaritan, and the King's Banquet.

Other Parts in the New Testament

- The **Acts of the Apostles** tells about the coming of the Holy Spirit and the beginning of the Christian community.
- **Letters** were written by many special people, especially Paul, who wrote to the Christian communities.
- The **Book of Revelation** was written to give hope to people who were suffering for their beliefs in Jesus.

Creed

I Believe

The **Creed** tells the faith of the Church. It brings together the Church's most important beliefs about

- God the Father, the Creator of all that is.
- Jesus, God's Son and the Savior.
- God the Holy Spirit, Giver of God's gifts.
- The Church, the Body of Christ in this world.

Nicene Creed

This creed which is prayed at Mass was written over a thousand years ago by leaders of the Church who met at a city named Nicaea. Christians over the centuries have prayed this creed.

Apostles' Creed

This creed gives a summary of the Apostles' beliefs. It is sometimes used at liturgies for children and is part of the Rosary.

The Twelve Apostles

Peter	Philip	Thaddeus
Andrew	Bartholomew	Thomas
James	Matthew	James
John	Simon	Judas

The Church

The Church is the community of the People of God. Like a human body, the Church has many parts, and the parts form one body. Christ is its head, and all Christians are its members. That is why the Church is called the Body of Christ.

The Church's Mission

Before his Ascension, when he returned to his Father in heaven, Jesus told his Apostles to take his message everywhere. The Church's work is to spread the good news of Jesus and God's kingdom throughout the world.

Members of the Church

Mary is the greatest of the saints because she said "yes" to being the Mother of God. She has many different titles and feast days.

Other holy people are also recognized as saints. They are remembered on special days in the Church year. These are called feast days.

Everlasting Life

The Church is also a sign of the glory of heaven meant for everyone. Christians believe that there is new life with God after life on earth.

Faith Fact

Catholics are required to attend Mass on holy days of obligation. The days that are called holy days in the United States are:

- Christmas, December 25
- Solemnity of Mary, Mother of God, January 1
- Ascension of the Lord, 40 days after Easter or the Seventh Sunday of Easter
- Assumption of Mary, August 15
- All Saints' Day, November 1
- Solemnity of the Immaculate Conception, December 8

Liturgy

The Sacraments

Catholics share in the worship of the Church by participating in the Church's sacraments. The Church has seven sacraments.

Sacrament	Description
Sacraments of Initiation	Baptism Confirmation Eucharist
Sacraments of Healing	Reconciliation Anointing of the Sick
Sacraments of Vocation and Service	Matrimony Holy Orders

One of the Sacraments of Healing is the **Sacrament of Reconciliation.** The Church knows that you do not always live as God wants you to live. So the Church provides the opportunity for you to experience God's love, mercy, and forgiveness in the Sacrament of Reconciliation. Through this sacrament, if you are sorry, God forgives any sins you have committed.

Faith Fact

When you are reconciled with God and others, you have peace.

Here is the word peace in different languages.

Arabic	salam
French	paix
German	frieden
Hebrew	shalom
Italian	pace
Tagalog	katahimikan
Spanish	paz
Vietnamese	hòa bình

Celebrating Reconciliation

God's gift of conscience helps you choose right from wrong. His gift of grace, God's life within, gives you the strength to do what is right. Review the steps for this celebration.

Step 1: Introductory rites

Step 2: Reading from Scripture

Step 3: Examination of conscience, litany of contrition, the Lord's Prayer

Step 4: Individual confession, penance, absolution

Step 5: Closing

Examination of Conscience

You prepare for the Sacrament of Reconciliation by thinking about how you keep God's Commandments and Jesus' law of love.

- Did I use God's name with respect?
- Did I show my love for God and others in some way?
- Did I usually say my daily prayers?
- Did I always obey my mother and father?
- Was I kind to those around me, or was I mean?
- Was I fair in the way that I played and worked with others?
- Did I share my things with others?
- Did I avoid taking what belongs to someone else?
- Did I care for my own things and others' things?
- Did I hurt others by calling them names or telling lies about them?
- Did I go to Mass and take part in the celebration?

Special Objects in Church

Altar The altar is the table where the Eucharist is celebrated.

Book of Gospels The Book of the Gospels contains the Gospel readings used at Mass.

Lectern (ambo) The lectern is a stand for announcing God's word in the readings at Mass.

Candles Candles lit during Mass are usually beeswax pillars. They show that Christ, the light of the world, is present.

Cruets Cruets are small bottles of water or wine.

Chalice The chalice is the cup for the Blood of Christ.

Tabernacle The tabernacle is a container where the Blessed Sacrament is kept for those who are homebound, sick, or dying, and at Mass.

Ciborium A ciborium is the special container placed in the tabernacle that holds the Eucharistic Bread, the Body of Christ.

Lectionary The lectionary is a special book used at Mass that contains readings from the Old and New Testament.

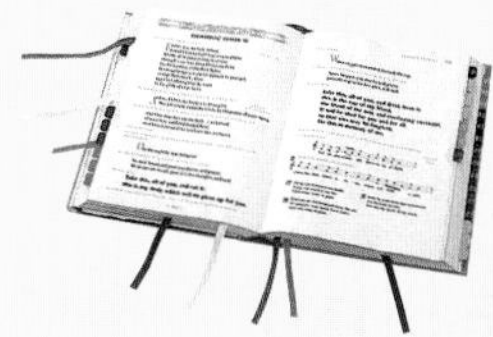

Roman Missal The Roman Missal is the special book that contains the prayers of the Mass.

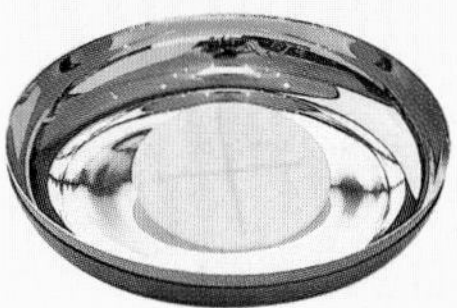

Paten The paten is the plate for the Body of Christ.

Sacrament of Eucharist

The Eucharist is a Sacrament of Initiation. It is the great thanksgiving prayer of Jesus and the Church. The Eucharist is the part of the Mass that is the Church's greatest act of worship and prayer to God. The Eucharist is also a sign of the heavenly feast that all are invited to at the end of time. The Eucharistic celebration always includes:

- proclamation of the word of God.
- thanksgiving to God for all his gifts.
- the consecration of bread and wine.
- receiving Christ's Body and Blood.

The Order of Mass

Introductory Rites

1. Entrance Chant
2. Greeting
3. Rite for the Blessing and Sprinkling of Water
4. Penitential Act
5. *Kyrie*
6. *Gloria*
7. Collect

Liturgy of the Word

The first great part of the Mass; the assembly listens to and responds to God's word in the Bible

1. First Reading (usually from the Old Testament)
2. Responsorial Psalm
3. Second Reading (from New Testament letters)
4. Gospel Acclamation (Alleluia)
5. Gospel Dialogue
6. Gospel Reading
7. Homily
8. Profession of Faith (Creed)
9. Prayer of the Faithful

Liturgy of the Eucharist

The second great part of the Mass; the Church offers thanks and praise to God

1. Preparation of the Gifts
2. Invitation to Prayer
3. Prayer over the Offerings
4. Eucharistic Prayer
   Preface Dialogue
   Preface
   Preface Acclamation
   Consecration
   Mystery of Faith
   Concluding Doxology
5. Communion Rite
   The Lord's Prayer
   Sign of Peace
   Lamb of God
   Invitation to Communion
   Communion
   Prayer After Communion

Concluding Rites

1. Greeting
2. Blessing
3. Dismissal

Receiving Holy Communion

When you receive Jesus in Holy Communion, you welcome him by showing reverence. These steps can help you.

- Fold your hands and join in the singing as you wait in line.
- When it is your turn, you can receive the Body of Christ in your hand or on your tongue.
- The person who offers you Communion will say, "The Body of Christ." You say, "Amen." Step aside, and chew and swallow the host.
- You may choose to drink from the cup. When the cup is offered to you, the person will say, "The Blood of Christ." You say, "Amen." Take a small sip.
- Return to your place in church. Pray quietly in your own words, thanking Jesus for being with you.

Because it is so important to have Jesus in your life in Holy Communion, the Church tells you to receive Communion frequently. The Church especially recommends that when you go to Mass, you should also receive Jesus in Communion.

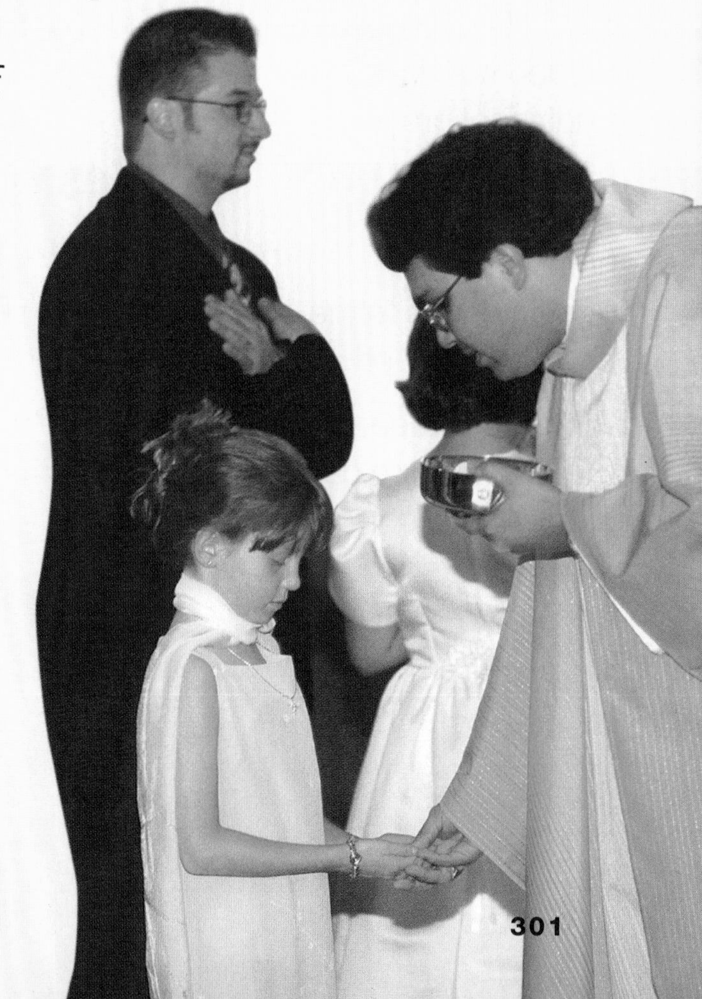

Liturgy

Sacramentals

As a reminder of Jesus' presence, the Church uses special signs and symbols. They are called sacramentals. A sacramental can be an object, words, or gestures.

Words

blessings
litanies
other prayers

Objects

crucifix
statues
holy water
candles
palms
rosary
images
medals

Gestures

Sign of the Cross
sign of peace
genuflection
procession

Faith Fact

A bow, a bending at the waist of the upper part of your body, or a reverent nod of your head is a gesture of reverence and worship.

Folded hands is a traditional prayer posture. It is a sign of prayerfulness, humility, and attentiveness to the presence of God.

When you kneel, you are in a posture of adoration or sorrow. When you stand, you are showing respect.

Images of Mary

Mary, the mother of Jesus, has a special place in the life of the Church. The Church honors her through special prayers, such as the Rosary, and through images, titles, and other prayers.

This stained-glass image of Mary is called "our Lady of the Blessed Sacrament."

This image of Mary comes from a church in Rome. It shows that Mary is "blessed among women" and blessed is the fruit of her womb, Jesus.

The Rosary

The rosary is a sacramental that reminds people of Mary, the mother of Jesus and that helps people reflect on the mysteries of Jesus' life and Mary's life.

Liturgy

The Church's Seasons

The **Church year** is a celebration of events in the life of Jesus. Every season of the Church's year has special feasts and colors and symbols.

Faith Fact

People from many countries bake Christmas cakes on the eve of the feast and eat them during the season. The cakes are thought to bring special blessings of health and good luck. Mexican *buñuelos* are unusual pastries baked of white flour, very crisp and brittle, and eaten with honey or syrup.

Advent

Christians prepare to celebrate God's coming in time through Jesus, and they also recall and await Christ's coming at the end of time.

Feasts: Immaculate Conception, Our Lady of Guadalupe

Color: violet

Symbols: Advent wreath, figure of John the Baptist

Christmas

The Church remembers the birth of Jesus and celebrates the coming in time of the Son of God.

Feasts: Christmas, Epiphany, Baptism of Jesus

Color: white or gold

Symbols: manger scenes, star of Bethlehem, Jesse tree

Ordinary Time

The Church celebrates the words and works of Jesus. Ordinary Time occurs twice in the year.

Feasts: Corpus Christi, Transfiguration, Solemnity of Christ the King

Color: green

Symbols: vine and branches, Good Shepherd

Lent

The Church recalls our baptismal promises to change our lives through prayer, fasting, and good works.

Feasts: Ash Wednesday, Palm Sunday

Color: violet (reddish-purple); red on Palm Sunday

Symbols: ashes, stations of the cross, palms

Easter Triduum

The three most holy days of the Church, when the Church remembers Jesus' passing from death to life.

Feasts: Holy Thursday, Good Friday, Holy Saturday, Easter

Color: white or gold and red (Good Friday)

Symbols: feet washing, veneration of cross, lighting the paschal candle

Easter Season

The Church celebrates Jesus' Resurrection and the new life that it brings to all.

Feasts: Ascension, Pentecost

Color: white or gold, red for Pentecost

Symbols: Alleluia, Easter lilies

God's Laws

God desires you to be in relationship with him. To help you do this and to know what is right, he has given you laws. God's laws include the Ten Commandments, the Great Commandment, Jesus' law of love, and the Beatitudes.

The Ten Commandments

THE TEN COMMANDMENTS	THEIR MEANING
1. I am the LORD your God: You shall not have strange Gods before me.	Keep God first in your life.
2. You shall not take the name of the LORD your God in vain.	Always use God's name in a reverent way.
3. Remember to keep holy the LORD's day.	Attend Mass and rest on Sunday.
4. Honor your father and your mother.	Obey your parents and guardians.
5. You shall not kill.	Care for yourself and others.
6. You shall not commit adultery.	Be respectful of every person.
7. You shall not steal.	Respect other people and their property.
8. You shall not bear false witness against your neighbor.	Respect others by always telling the truth.
9. You shall not covet your neighbor's wife.	Don't be jealous of other people's friendships.
10. You shall not covet your neighbor's goods.	Don't be jealous of what other people have.

The Great Commandment

"You shall love the Lord your God with all your heart, with all your soul, with all your strength, and with all your mind, and your neighbor as yourself."

Luke 10:27

The Beatitudes

Blessed are the poor in spirit,
for theirs is the kingdom of heaven.
Blessed are they who mourn,
for they will be comforted.
Blessed are the meek,
for they will inherit the land.
Blessed are they who hunger and thirst
for righteousness,
for they will be satisfied.
Blessed are the merciful,
for they will be shown mercy.
Blessed are the clean of heart,
for they will see God.
Blessed are the peacemakers,
for they will be called children of God.
Blessed are they who are persecuted for
the sake of righteousness,
for theirs is the kingdom of heaven.

Matthew 5: 3-10

Faith Fact

Symbols that represent the theological virtues are:

cross → faith

anchor → hope

heart → love

Law of Love

"This is my commandment: love one another as I have loved you."

John 15:12

Virtues

God's grace within you helps you grow in virtue. Virtues are good spiritual habits that strengthen you and enable you to do what is right and good. The theological virtues are faith, hope, and love.

The Lord's Prayer

Our Father,
who art in heaven,
hallowed be thy name;
thy kingdom come,
thy will be done on earth
as it is in heaven.
Give us this day our daily bread;
and forgive us our trespasses
as we forgive those who trespass
against us;
and lead us not into temptation,
but deliver us from evil. Amen.

Hail, Mary

Hail, Mary, full of grace.
The Lord is with you!
Blessed are you among women,
and blessed is the fruit of your womb, Jesus.
Holy Mary, Mother of God,
pray for us sinners,
now and at the hour of our death. Amen.

The Jesus Prayer

Lord Jesus Christ, Son of God,
have mercy upon me, a sinner.

Glory to the Father

Glory to the Father, and to the Son,
and to the Holy Spirit.
As it was in the beginning, is now,
and will be for ever. Amen.

Act of Contrition

My God, I am sorry for my sins
with all my heart.
In choosing to do wrong
and failing to do good,
I have sinned against you
whom I should love above all things.
I firmly intend, with your help,
to do penance, to sin no more,
and to avoid whatever leads me to sin.
Our Savior Jesus Christ
suffered and died for us.
In his name, my God, have mercy.

Act of Faith, Hope, and Love

My God, I believe in you, I hope in you,
I love you above all things, with all my mind
and heart and strength.

Prayer

The Apostles' Creed

I believe in God,
the Father almighty,
Creator of heaven and earth,
and in Jesus Christ, his only Son, our Lord,

At the words that follow, up to and including
the Virgin Mary, *all bow.*

who was conceived by the Holy Spirit,
born of the Virgin Mary,
suffered under Pontius Pilate,
was crucified, died and was buried;
he descended into hell;
on the third day he rose again from the dead;

he ascended into heaven,
and is seated at the right hand
of God the Father almighty;
from there he will come to judge
the living and the dead.

I believe in the Holy Spirit,
the holy catholic Church,
the communion of saints,
the forgiveness of sins,
the resurrection of the body,
and life everlasting. Amen.

Faith Fact

When a pope is elected, he is given a ring with a figure of Saint Peter fishing on it. This reminds the pope that he is to be a leader of God's people as Peter was.

Angel Guardian (contemporary)

Angel sent by God to guide me,
be my light and walk beside me;
be my guardian and protect me;
on the path of life direct me.

Angel Guardian (traditional)

Angel of God,
my Guardian dear,
to whom his love commits
me here,
ever this day (night)
be at my side,
to light and guard,
to rule and guide.

Faith Fact

An angel is a messenger of God. Angels are mentioned nearly 300 times in the Bible. Three important angels are Gabriel, Michael, and Raphael.

Rev. Peter Klein,
The Catholic Source Book

Grace Before Meals

Bless us, O Lord, and these
your gifts
which we are about to receive
from your goodness, through
Christ our Lord. Amen.

Grace After Meals

We give you thanks for all your
gifts, almighty God,
living and reigning now and
forever. Amen.

Morning Prayer

Blessed are you, Lord, God of all creation:
you take the sleep from my eyes
and the slumber from my eyelids.
Amen.

Evening Prayer

Protect us, Lord, as we stay awake;
watch over us as we sleep,
that awake, we may keep watch with Christ,
and asleep, rest in his peace.
Amen.

Grace Before Mealtime

Loving God, all that we have
comes from your goodness
and the work of those who love us.
Bless us and the food we share.
Watch over those who care for us.
Open our eyes to the needs of the poor.
We ask this through Christ our Lord.
Amen.

Grace After Mealtime

We give you thanks, Almighty God,
for all your gifts
which we have received,
through Christ our Lord. Amen.

Faith Fact

We also say a prayer at mealtime. We call this "saying grace." We thank God for giving us food to eat. We ask him to bless the food so we grow and stay healthy. We remember people who don't have enough to eat.

See page 311 for more mealtime prayers.

Faith Fact

In times of sadness it is good to pray. God will heal you and comfort you if you ask him. You can pray for someone else who is sad or suffering.

See page 309 for an example of a prayer of sorrow called an Act of Contrition.

Prayer of Sorrow

Most holy and most merciful God,
strength of the weak,
rest for the weary,
comfort of the sorrowful.

[The Lord says:]
Do not fear, for I am with you.
Do not be afraid, for I am your God;
I will strengthen you, I will help you,
I will hold you in my hand. [Cf.] *Isaiah* 41:10

Prayer for the Suffering

Lord Jesus Christ, source of our life,
heal the suffering
and comfort the brokenhearted.

Prayer of Community Petition

God of love, our strength and protection, hear the prayer of your Church.
Grant that when we come to you in faith, our prayers may be answered, through Christ our Lord.
Amen.

Prayer of Petition

Lord God, you know our weakness.
In your mercy grant that the example of your saints may bring us back to love and serve you through Christ our Lord.
Amen.

Birthday Blessing

Loving God,
you created all the people of the world,
and you know each of us by name.
We thank you for N.,
who celebrates his/her birthday.
Bless him/her with your love and friendship
that he/she may grow in wisdom, knowledge,
and grace.
May he/she love his/her family always
and be ever faithful to his/her friends.
Grant this through Christ our Lord.
Amen.

School Blessing

Lord God,
fill this room (school, church)
with kindness for one another
and with respect for guests.
Teach us to welcome everyone
without judgment or prejudice
but with Christian joy.
Fill us with true wisdom
which is to seek Jesus always,
now and for ever.
Amen.

Prayer for Saint Joseph's Day

Almighty God,
in your wisdom and love
you chose Joseph to be the husband of Mary,
the mother of your Son.
As we enjoy his protection on earth
may we have the help of his prayers in heaven.
We ask this through Christ our Lord.
Amen.

Prayer for Saint Valentine's Day

God our Creator,
bless the love that brings people together
and grows ever stronger in our hearts.
May all the messages that carry the name
of your holy Bishop Valentine
be sent in good joy
and received in delight.
We ask this through Christ our Lord.
Amen.

Faith Fact

When we pray with the saints, we ask them to pray to God for us and to pray with us. The saints are with Christ. They speak for us when we need help.

Prayer of Saint Francis

Lord, make me an instrument of your peace;
where there is hatred, let me sow love;
where there is injury, pardon;
where there is doubt, faith;
where there is despair, hope;
where there is darkness, light;
and where there is sadness, joy.

Litanies

Christ, hear us.
Christ, graciously hear us.
Lord Jesus, hear our prayer.
Lord Jesus, hear our prayer.

Holy Mary, Mother of God, **pray for us**
Saint John the Baptist, **pray for us**
Saint Joseph, **pray for us**
Saint Peter and Saint Paul, **pray for us**

Faith Fact

A litany is a prayer with one line that is meant to be repeated over and over again so that those praying are caught up in the prayer itself.

Lord, have mercy.
Lord, have mercy.
Christ have mercy.
Christ have mercy.
Lord have mercy.
Lord have mercy.

Sign of the Cross

In English
In the name of the Father,
and of the Son,
and of the Holy Spirit.
Amen.

In Latin
In nomine Patris,
et Filii,
et Spiritus Sancti.
Amen.

Glory to the Father

In English
Glory to the Father,
and to the Son,
and to the Holy Spirit:
as it was in the beginning,
is now,
and will be forever. Amen.

In Latin
Gloria Patri,
et Filio,
et Spiritui Sancto.
Sicut erat in principio,
et nunc, et semper,
et in saecula saeculorum. Amen.

Words of Faith

A

absolution The forgiveness of sin you receive from God through the Church in the Sacrament of Reconciliation. *(163)*

adore Worship God. Adoration is a form of prayer. *(208)*

Advent The season of four weeks before Christmas. During Advent the Church prepares to celebrate the birth of Jesus. *(170)*

assembly The people gathered together for worship. *(223)*

Baptism The sacrament that makes the person a child of God and a member of the Church. It takes away original sin and all personal sin. *(151)*

Bible The word of God written in human words. There are two parts to the Bible, the Old Testament and the New Testament. *(63)*

Church The community of all baptized people who believe in God and follow Jesus. The word is often used for the Catholic Church. *(101)*

Church year The celebration in the liturgy of events in the life of Jesus. *(170)*

conscience A gift from God that helps you know right from wrong. *(126–127)*

consecration Through the power of the Holy Spirit and the words and actions of the priest, the gifts of bread and wine become the Body and Blood of Jesus. *(245)*

contrition Being sorry for sin and wanting to live better. *(161)*

creation Everything made by God. *(42–43)*

creed A statement of the Church's beliefs. *(235)*

disciples People who choose to follow Jesus. *(100-101)*

Easter The Church's celebration of the Resurrection of Jesus from the dead. The celebrations at the Easter Vigil on Holy Saturday and on Easter Sunday mark the Church's greatest holy day, Easter. *(173)*

Eucharist The sacrament in which Jesus shares himself and the bread and wine become his Body and Blood. *(222)*

Eucharistic Prayer The great prayer of thanksgiving prayed by the priest in your name and that of the Church. *(245)*

faith Belief in God and all that he has told about himself. *(187)*

God the Father A name for God that tells God's great love for people. God the Father is the first Person of the Holy Trinity. *(81)*

God the Holy Spirit The third Person in the Holy Trinity. The Holy Spirit is a guide who helps people stay close to God. *(101)*

grace A sharing in God's life. *(151)*

Great Commandment Jesus' law to love God above all else and to love others the way you love yourself. It sums up all God's laws. *(115)*

heaven Life and happiness forever with God. *(278)*

holy From God or something that shows what God is like. *(259)*

Holy Communion Holy Bread and Wine that you receive in Eucharist. *(261)*

Holy Family The name for Jesus, Mary, and Joseph. *(90–91)*

Holy Trinity A name for the three Persons in one God—Father, Son, and Holy Spirit. *(99)*

homily A short talk about the readings at Mass. *(234)*

Kingdom of God Love, peace, and justice for all. *(188–189)*

Last Supper The meal Jesus shared with his followers on the night before he died. *(245)*

Lent The season of forty days during which the Church gets ready for Easter. It is a time of prayer, good actions, and sorrow for sin. Lent begins with Ash Wednesday. *(172)*

liturgy The public worship of the Church. It includes the Sacraments and forms of daily prayer. *(170–171)*

Liturgy of the Eucharist The second main part of the Mass. *(245)*

Liturgy of the Word The first main part of the Mass. *(233)*

Lord's Prayer The prayer that Jesus taught his followers to pray to God the Father. *(207)*

Mass Another name for the celebration of the Sacrament of the Eucharist. *(222–223)*

mercy Loving kindness and forgiveness. *(136–137)*

mission The work of the Church. *(269)*

missionaries People who bring the Good News of Jesus and God's kingdom to people in other places. *(269)*

Mortal sins Serious sins that cut people off from God's life. *(127)*

New Testament The second part of the Bible that tells of the life and teaching of Jesus, his followers, and the early Church. *(65)*

Old Testament The first part of the Bible that is about God and his people before Jesus was born. *(63)*

original sin The first sin committed by the first people. *(53)*

parable Short stories about everyday life. *(232–233)*

penance A prayer or an act to make up for sin. *(163)*

Pentecost The day the Holy Spirit first came upon the disciples and the Church. *(173)*

praise Giving God honor and thanks because he is good. Praise is a form of prayer. *(42)*

prayer Talking to and listening to God. *(81)*

Prayer of the Faithful Prayer at Mass for the needs of the Church and the world. *(235)*

proclaim To tell about Jesus with loving words and actions. *(197)*

psalm A prayer from the Bible; it can be said or sung. *(42)*

reverence The care and respect you show to God and holy persons and things. *(261)*

Resurrection The mystery of Jesus being raised from death. *(173)*

sacrament A holy sign that comes from Jesus and gives life. *(151)*

sacramentals Blessings, objects, and actions that remind you of God and are made sacred through the prayers of the Church. *(209)*

Sacraments of Initiation The first sacraments that are celebrated by new members of the Church: Baptism, Confirmation, and Eucharist. *(153)*

Sacrament of Reconciliation The sacrament in which God's forgiveness for sin is given through the Church. *(162–163)*

sacrifice Giving up something out of love for someone else or for the common good. Jesus sacrificed his life for all people. *(242)*

saint A holy person who obeyed God and followed Jesus. *(79)*

Savior The one sent into the world to save people who were lost through sin and to lead people back to God. *(54–55)*

sin Choosing to disobey God. It is doing what you know is wrong. *(44–45)*

Son of God The name of Jesus that tells you God is his Father. *(45)*

Temple The holy building in Jerusalem where the Jewish people came to worship God. *(90–91)*

Ten Commandments God's laws about loving God and others. *(114–115)*

The Three Days The most holy time of the Church year—Holy Thursday, Good Friday, Holy Saturday, and Easter Sunday. It celebrates Jesus' passing through death to life. *(28)*

trust To believe in and depend on someone. *(81)*

Venial sins Less serious sins that do not completely remove a person from God's life and love. *(127)*

Illustration Credits
Paul Bachem 42-43, 91; Dan Brown 90, 98-99, 197, 222-223; David Cabot 68-69; Olivia Cole 45, 101, 173, 175, 245, 247; Carolyn Croll 20-21, 102; Bob Dombrowski 62-63; Allen Eitzen 32-33; Barbara Kiwak 44-45, 88-89, 188-189; Dennis Lyall 36-37; Geoff McCormack 270-271; Diane Paterson 12-13, 127, 139, 270; Karen Patkau 52-53; 232-233; Roger Payne 8-9, 124-125, 278-279; Frances-ca Pelizzoli 100; Larry Schwinger 80-81, 92-93, 92-93, 134-135, 186-187; Bill SMITH STUDIO 46, 56, 92, 118, 119, 155, 164, 174, 210, 211, 282; Joel Spector 54-55; Clive Spong 160-161, 258-259, 268-269; Arvis Stewart 24-25, 116-117, 195, 201, 242-243; Matt Straub 43, 46, 47, 50, 60, 79, 82, 103, 108, 109, 115, 119, 125, 128, 129, 137, 138, 138, 142, 144, 145, 153, 155, 158, 165, 171, 174, 181, 189, 190, 191, 194, 200, 211, 217, 223, 227, 235, 236, 250, 252, 253, 263, 271, 273, 283, 287, 288; Walter Stuart 114, 196-197; Susan Swan, 152; Meryl Treatner 150-151; Douglas Van Fleet 20-21; Lois Woolley 50, 60, 70, 86, 96, 106, 122, 132, 142, 158, 168, 178, 194, 204, 214, 230, 250, 266, 276, 286; The Curator Collection, Ltd. 190.

Photo Credits
iv Ariel Skelley/Blend Images/Corbis; 1 l Jo Foord/DK Images; 1 r Rubberball Productions/ Getty Images; 2 Jon Feingersch/Masterfile; 6-7 bg Myrleen Ferguson Cate/Photo Edit; 7 inset Father Gene Plaisted, OSC; 10-11 bg LF File/Shutterstock Images LLC; 11 t Photodisc/Getty Images; 11 b Tom & Dee Ann McCarthy/Corbis; 14-15 bg Sally Brown/Index Stock Imagery/Photolibrary; 15 bg Corel; 15 fg Richard Hutchings; 16-17 bg Hans Georg Roth/Corbis; 16-17 fg SW Productions/Getty Images; 18-19 Richard Hutchings/Corbis; 22-23 fg Richard Hutchings; 22-23 bg Mitchell Funk/Getty Images; 26-27 bg Corel; 27 bl Photos.com; 27 br Stephen Simpson/Getty Images; 28-29 Stephanie Maze/Corbis; 30-31 bg Stephanie Maze/Corbis; 31 fg Richard Hutchings; 34-35 bg Bryan F. Peterson/ Corbis; 35 inset Stockbyte/Getty Images; 38-39 Roger Tidman/Corbis; 40 l Adamsmith/ Getty Images; 40 c Lisette Le Bon/SuperStock; 40 r Jon Feingersch/Masterfile; 40-41 bg Adamsmith/Getty Images; 45 Steve Satushek; 47 t KEITA SAWAKI/a.collectionRF/Getty Images; 47 c Eva Ritchie/Getty Images; 47 b Getty Images; 48 Raoul Minsart; 51 Lisette Le Bon/SuperStock; 56 Dave Nagel/Getty Images; 57 t LWA-Dann Tardif/CORBIS; 57 b Banana Stock/Punchstock; 58 Neil Beer/ Photodisc/Getty Images; 61 Jon Feingersch/ Masterfile; 63 Creatas/Age Fotostock; 65 Our Sunday Visitor Curriculum Division; 66 Comstock/Jupiter Images; 68 Myrdal Mase/ Getty Images; 71 t Louise Tanguay; 71 bl Tom Stewart/Corbis; 71 bc Myrleen Ferguson Cate/PhotoEdit; 71 br Michael Newman/ PhotoEdit; 71 bg Stuart Westmorland/Corbis; 72 t fivespots/Shutterstock Images LLC; 72 bl Juice Images/Corbis; 73 fg David Laronde/ Corbis; 73 bg Stuart Westmorland/Corbis; 76 l AJA Productions/Getty Images; 76 c Daniel Pangbourne/Getty Images; 76 r Zave Smith/ Age Fotostock; 76-77 bg AJA Productions/ Getty Images; 79 Photo Courtesy of Salesian Missions; 82 Ariel Skelley/Blend Images/ Corbis; 84 Jose Luis Pelaez, Inc./Corbis; 87 Daniel Pangbourne/Getty Images; 89 David Young-Wolff/PhotoEdit; 94 Richard Hutchings; 96 Catherine Yeulet/iStock; 97 Zave Smith/Age Fotostock; 99 t Myrleen Ferguson Cate/PhotoEdit; 99 b Father Gene Plaisted, OSC; 101 Michael Keller/Corbis; 102-103 Index Stock/Photolibrary; 104 Bill Wittman; 106 SW Productions/Punchstock; 107 t Bill Aron/PhotoEdit; 107 b Kevin Radford/Masterfile; 107 bg Frank Krahmer/ Getty Images; 108-109 James Shaffer/ PhotoEdit; 112 l Charlie Edwards/Photodisc/ Getty Images; 112 c Graham French/ Masterfile; 112 r Kevin Dodge/Masterfile; 112-114 bg Charlie Edwards/Photodisc/ Getty Images; 115 Philip Gould/Corbis; 117 Richard Hutchings; 120 Banana Stock, Ltd./ Punchstock; 123 Graham French/Masterfile; 126 Raoul Minsart/Masterfile; 128 rubberball/ Getty Images; 130 Bill Wittman; 132 Nancy Sheehan/Index Stock Imagery/Photolibrary; 133 Kevin Dodge/Masterfile; 136 Richard Hutchings; 137 Richard Hutchings; 138 t Tony Anderson/Getty Images; 138 b Bryan Allen/CORBIS; 140 Father Gene Plaisted, OSC; 143 t Adrian Arbib/Corbis; 143 b Bill Aron/ PhotoEdit; 145 Reed Kaestner/Corbis; 148 l Stockbyte/Getty Images; 148 c Photodisc/ Getty Images; 148 r Justin Pumfrey/Carrie Beecroft/Getty Images; 148-149 bg Stockbyte/ Getty Images; 151 t Father Gene Plaisted, OSC; 151 b Ryan McVay/Getty Images; 153 Father Gene Plaisted, OSC; 154 Bob Thomas/ Getty Images; 156 Father Gene Plaisted, OSC; 159 Photodisc/Getty Images; 161 t Bill Wittman; 161 b Andreas Kuehn/Getty Images; 162 l Father Gene Plaisted, OSC; 162 r Bill Wittman; 163 Myrleen Ferguson Cate/PhotoEdit; 164 Myrleen Ferguson Cate/ PhotoEdit; 166 Michael Keller/Corbis; 168 ULTRA.F/Digital Vision/Getty Images; 169 Justin Pumfrey/Carrie Beecroft/Getty Images; 170 Richard Hutchings; 171 t Peter Holmes/ Age Fotostock; 171 b Burke/Triolo/Brand X Pictures/Punchstock; 172 Richard Hutchings; 173 Father Gene Plaisted, OSC; 176 Rubberball Productions; 178 Jeff Greenberg/Index Stock Imagery/Photolibrary; 179 t Jose Luis Pelaez, Inc./Corbis; 179 b Richard Hutchings/ PhotoEdit; 179 bg VisionsofAmerica/Joe Sohm/Getty Images; 180-181 Randy Taylor/ Index Stock/Photolibrary; 184 l Richard Hutchings; 184 c Dan Lim/Masterfile; 184 r Richard Hutchings; 184-185 bg Richard Hutchings; 189 Myrleen Ferguson Cate/ PhotoEdit; 192 Kevin Dodge/Masterfile; 195 Dan Lim/Masterfile; 198 t Alvaro Leiva/Age Fotostock; 198 c Paul Barton/Corbis; 198 b Arthur Tilley/Getty Images; 199 l Father Gene Plaisted, OSC; 199 r Bill Wittman; 202 David Noton; 204 Gabrielle Revere/Getty Images; 205 Richard Hutchings; 206 Bill Wittman; 208 t Frank Siteman/Getty Images; 208 b Thinkstock/Getty Images; 209 Jim Corwin/Index Stock Imagery/Photolibrary; 210 Geostock/Getty Images; 212 Michael Newman/PhotoEdit; 214 Myrleen Ferguson Cate/PhotoEdit; 215 Digital Vision/Getty Images; 216 c Alyx Kellington/Index Stock/ Photolibrary; 216 bl Michele Burgess/Index Stock/Photolibrary; 216 br Peter Turnley/ Corbis; 220 l Ronnie Kaufman/CORBIS; 220 c David Pollack/CORBIS; 220 r David Schmidt/ Masterfile; 220-221 bg Ronnie Kaufman/ CORBIS; 223 Bill Wittman; 224 Father Gene Plaisted, OSC; 225 Richard Hutchings; 226 Tony Freeman/PhotoEdit; 228 Kevin Dodge/ Masterfile; 230 Stuart Pearce/AgeFotostock; 231 David Pollack/CORBIS; 233 t Bill Wittman; 233 b Myrleen Ferguson Cate/PhotoEdit; 234 Father Gene Plaisted, OSC; 235 Bill Wittman; 237 Andy Crawford/DK Images; 238 Digital Vision/Getty Images; 241 David Schmidt/Masterfile; 243 Bill Wittman; 244 Myrleen Ferguson Cate/PhotoEdit; 245 Father Gene Plaisted, OSC; 246 Michael Newman/ PhotoEdit; 248 A & F Pears, Ltd., London/ SuperStock; 251 t Mark Richards/PhotoEdit; 251 b Hutchings Stock Photography/CORBIS; 252 Royalty-Free/Corbis; 256 l Jose Luis Pelaez, Inc./CORBIS; 256 c Massis J. Boujikian/ Corbis; 256 r Roger Tully/Getty Images; 256-257 bg Jose Luis Pelaez, Inc./CORBIS; 259 Father Gene Plaisted, OSC; 260 Spencer Grant/PhotoEdit; 261 Myrleen Ferguson Cate/PhotoEdit; 262 t Myrleen Ferguson Cate/PhotoEdit; 262 b Bill Wittman; 264 Bill Wittman; 266 Burke/Triolo Productions/Getty Images; 267 fg Massis J. Boujikian/Corbis; 267 bg The Copyright Group/SuperStock ; 269 Victor Maqque/Courtesy Maryknoll Mission Archives; 271 bg Courtesy of Missionary Sisters of the Sacred Heart of Jesus Stella Maris Province, New York City; 271 fg C Squared Studios/Photodisc/Getty Images; 272 Paul Conklin/PhotoEdit; 274 Bill Wittman; 276 David Young-Wolff/PhotoEdit; 277 Roger Tully/Getty Images; 280 Bill Wittman; 281 tl SW Productions/Getty Images; 281 br Myrleen Ferguson Cate/PhotoEdit; 282 Corbis; 284 Digital Vision/Getty Images; 286 Rick Gomez/ Masterfile; 287 t Myrleen Ferguson Cate/ PhotoEdit; 288 Barbara A. Creed; 292-293 Richard Hutchings; 294 KAI PFAFFENBACH/ Reuters/Corbis; 296 NASA-GSFC; 298 tl Digital Imaging Group; 298 tr Digital Imaging Group; 298 tcl Digital Imaging Group; 298 tcr Digital Imaging Group; 298 bcl Digital Imaging Group; 298 bcr Digital Imaging Group; 298 bl Digital Imaging Group; 298 br Digital Imaging Group; 299tl Digital Imaging Group; 299 tr Digital Imaging Group; 299 b Digital Imaging Group; 301 Bill Wittman; 302 t Photos.com; 302 c Photodisc/Getty Images; 302 b Richard Hutchings; 303 t Father Gene Plaisted, OSC; 303 b Arte & Immagini srl/Corbis; 304 l Father Gene Plaisted, OSC; 304 r Photos.com; 305 l Corel; 305 r Corel; 307 PhotoSpin; 308-309 Thinkstock/ Getty Images; 310-311 Thinkstock/Getty Images; 312-313 Thinkstock/Getty Images; 314-315 Thinkstock/Getty Images; 316-317 Thinkstock/Getty Images; 318-319 Thinkstock/Getty Images

Acknowledgments
For permission to reprint copyrighted material, grateful acknowledgment is made to the following sources:

International Consultation on English Texts: English translation of Glory to the Father (*the Gloria Patri*), Lord, have mercy, the Apostles' Creed, the Lord's Prayer, Lamb of God (*Agnus Dei*), and *Kyrie eleison* by the International Consultation on English Texts (ICET).

The Liturgical Conference: Adapted from "February 14, Saint Valentine's Day" (Retitled: "Prayer for St. Valentine's Day") in *Major Feasts and Seasons.*

Liturgy Training Publications, 1800 North Hermitage Avenue, Chicago, IL 60622, 1-800-933-1800, www.ltp.org: From "Meal Prayer for Harvest Time" (Retitled: "Grace Before Mealtime"), "Prayers for Sad Days" (Retitled: "Prayer of Sorrow"), "Prayer for Times of Crisis" (Retitled: "Prayer for the Suffering") and "Epiphany Blessing of a Gathering Space" (Retitled: "School Blessings") in *Blessings and Prayers through the Year: A Resource for School and Parish* by Elizabeth McMahon Jeep. Text © 2004 by Archdiocese of Chicago.

Twenty-Third Publications, A Division of Bayard: "Grace After Meals" (Retitled: "Grace After Mealtime") from *500 Prayers for Catholic Schools & Parish Youth Groups* by Filomena Tassi and Peter Tassi. Text copyright © 2004 by Filomena Tassi and Peter Tassi.

United States Conference of Catholic Bishops, Inc., Washington, D.C.: "At Bedside" (Retitled: "Evening Prayer") and "Washing and Dressing" (Retitled: "Morning Prayer") from *Catholic Household Blessings and Prayers.* Translation copyright © 1989 by United States Catholic Conference, Inc. From the English translation of "Blessing on Birthdays or the Anniversary of Baptism" (Retitled: "Birthday Blessing") in *Book of Blessings.* Translation copyright © 1988 by United States Catholic Conference, Inc.

"With a Little Help" by Katie Bahr; used with permission from Arlington Catholic Herald, catholicherald.com.